Finding
Slovenia

FINDING SLOVENIA
Text by Jacqueline Widmar Stewart

Proofreader Peter Waller
Editor Senja Požar
Designer and artwork Klemen Kunaver
Production Marko Prah
Photo on the cover Klemen Kunaver

Chairman of the Managing Board Milan Matos
Executive Director of Publishing Department Tina Škerlj

Mladinska knjiga Založba, d.d., Ljubljana
Printed by Euroadria

Ljubljana, 2009
First edition, printrun 3,500 copies

Photographs and maps contributed by: Marjan Garbajs: p. 27, 90. Aleksandar Hajdukovič: p. 178. Jože Hanc: p. 134, 154. Tomo Jeseničnik: p. 41, 45, 49, 50, 58, 67, 71, 88, 93, 96, 101d, 112, 113, 117, 133, 138, 149, 150, 161, 163, 164, 165, 166, 168, 169, 170, 172, 173, 175, 179. Milan Kambič: p. 45, 92, 99, 100, 119. Stane Klemenc: p. 51, 66, 95, 98, 130, 131. Mitja Košir: p. 43. Simon Kržič: p. 106. Tomaž Lanko: p. 91u. Matevž Lenarčič: p. 55. Tomi Lombar: p. 24l. Maps: Monde Neuf, MKZ. MKZ photographs: p. 16, 17, 20, 24r, 25, 29r, 42, 48d, 52, 57, 60, 61, 75, 80, 81u,d, 98, 99, 101, 152, 153 (STV p. 82, 85, 86, 91, 93, 97, 105, 135, 144, 176). Narodna galerija v Ljubljani: p. 103d. Franci Novak: p. 6, 14, 18, 35, 48, 72, 104, 122, 123, 132, 143, 148, 171. I.Piry, B. Grafenauer: p. 32. Pokrajinski muzej Celje: p. 28. Edo Primožič: p. 29l. Marko Pršina: p. 57. Jure Senegačnik: p. 47, 64, 78, 83, 107, 111, 114, 115d, u; 116, 118, 121, 124, 129, 147, 127, 128, 141. Marjan Smerke: p. 33. Tomislav Stajduhar: p. 46. Milan Štupar: p. 27l. Matej Vranič: p. 44. Dunja Wedam: p. 29r, 54, 142. Dušan Zidar: p. 151.

In case we did not state the right source of certain picture/photo, we will do this in the re-print of this edition.

CIP - Kataložni zapis o publikaciji
Narodna in univerzitetna knjižnica, Ljubljana

908(497.4)
913(497.4)(036)

WIDMAR Stewart, Jacqueline
    Finding Slovenia : a guide to old Europe's new country / [text
by Jacqueline Widmar Stewart]. - Ljubljana : Mladinska knjiga, 2009

ISBN 978-961-01-0851-1

245669376

Finding Slovenia

A Guide to Old Europe's New Country

Mladinska knjiga
PUBLISHING HOUSE

Ljubljana • Zagreb • Beograd • Sarajevo
Skopje • Bukarešta

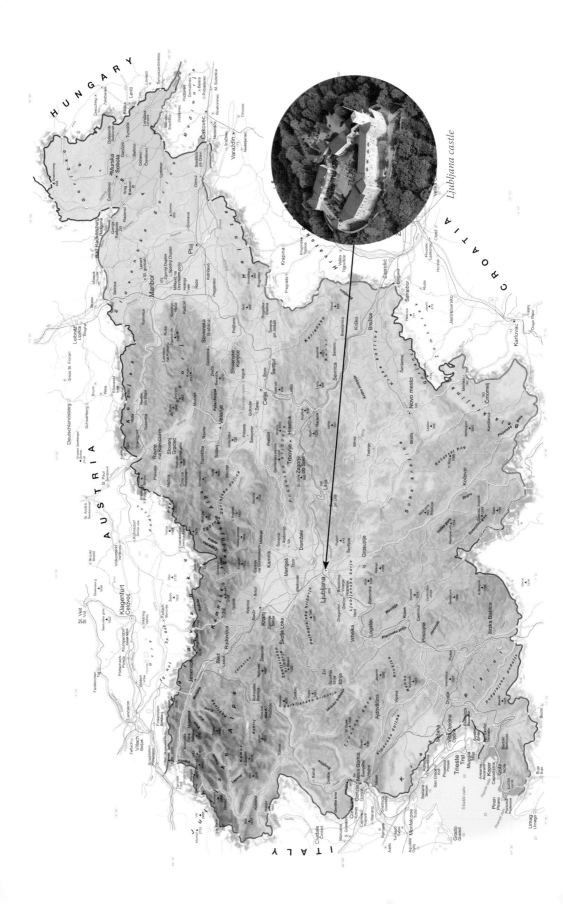

Ljubljana castle

Foreword

This book doesn't pretend to be either unbiased or complete.

My objective is to acquaint you with a land of people who have achieved long-sought independence in a land of stunning natural beauty.

Some history comes first, with a timeline and examples of castle museums.

An overview of physical features follows. Parklands, footpaths, and hot spring spas can keep you fit as you move through exquisite scenery.

For purposes of organization, the next section splits Slovenia into five areas and highlights places in each that might be of particular interest to you.

First comes Ljubljana, then each of the four corners of the country followed by sample itineraries.

The planning chapter encourages you to tailor your trip and benefit from local expertise.

How to find food is key to your experience. Some words and signals are given to guide you.

Have no fear in your search. The locals will help you.

Food is of major importance to Slovenians.

You can find wineries just about everywhere. A few of the better-known regions are indicated. Your lodging can be a mountain hut or a castle. A peek inside a couple of them may help you choose.

This book is intended to help you celebrate with Slovenians by sharing their culture, parklands, wines, foods and fun.

May your paths be captivating and your palate enthralled in this land of varied treasures.

Introduction

I have not watched this country's recent triumphs with dispassionate detachment. My Slovenian grandparents fled Central Europe's poverty and oppression at the turn of the 20th century. It took until 1967 for my fully-Americanized parents and I, shaking with fear, to make our way back across the Austrian border into the then Yugoslavia, despite dire warnings about bandits waiting there to kidnap and strip us of all our earthly goods.

Instead we were met with uncommon kindness, generosity and ready laughter. It soon became clear that the real challenge is how to keep a Slovenian from giving. If you look confused on the street, you'll be offered direction instantaneously. Come close to anyone's country home and you'll be plied with homemade bread, sausage, wine and schnapps.

Slovenians love their land and want to tell you about it. They can name each rivelet with its source and destination, and each peak with its height, access and climbing time. "If you haven't climbed Triglav, you are not Slovenian."

At 9,397 feet, the highest peak in the Julian Alps gives its name to Triglav National Park. You might think of the park as a Slovenian Yosemite with a liberal sprinkling of mountain huts. In the hiking season you can easily find hearty mountain fare, beverages, and quite often some alpine serenading.

Two aspects of life here will add to the pleasure of your trip. Slovenians are devoted to education and the environment. Throughout their history, they have sought the right to speak their own language and to have an educational system. Much effort has gone into the preservation of natural resources.

Breathtaking scenery easily enjoyable by foot, ski, bike or car provides reason enough to visit the little centrally-situated sovereignty. But there is more. The same forces that

- Slovenian forbears probably came to present-day Slovenia in the 600s, about 1,000 years before the English settled in New England.
- Not until more than thirteen hundred years later, in 1991, did Slovenians win their long-coveted independence.
- In 2004, the new Republic of Slovenia gained admittance to the European Union, and in 2008 held the EU presidency.

< Triglav, the highest mountain in Slovenia, 9,397 feet above sea level

As you travel around Slovenia, think of the tales the hills could tell you. Share the awe of natural wonder; tread the trails, but as you wander,

honor the age-old endeavors to be literate, informed, democratic and free.

shaped the Slovenian landscape brought thermal mineral springs.

Vital to Roman life and later to elite European resorts, the "toplice," (warm waters) continue to offer restorative opportunities. While weeklong stays were most typical in the past, modern facilities also offer drop-in services for shorter periods. This means that you can swim, avail yourself of water and air massage in indoor and outdoor pools of varying temperatures, and choose lodging and dining on-site or elsewhere.

You have great scenery that you savor with fresh food, drink and hospitality. You have hot springs that keep you relaxed and healthy, and there is still more.

Slovenia offers a broad range of cultural opportunities too. The castles that grace Slovenia's cities and promontories often house museums. In Ljubljana, Celje, Kranj, Piran, Skofja Loka, Ptuj, Novo mesto, Metlika, Ribnica, and Murska Sobota you will find fascinating architecture and displays, sometimes dating back to Roman times. In cities like Ljubljana and Maribor, you can attend a concert, the theater, ballet, musical performances, and art exhibitions. The land is full of surprises. Tiny villages often offer big festivals.

For comprehensive, detailed information, please consult the web and other guides. This book is meant to help you find this marvelous place, but then to chart your own course within it. Please see the section on tourist services for information on tailoring your own trip, with or without professional guides.

Table of Contents

The Essence of Slovenia

The Last 62,000 Years

T o make a long history more digestible, it has been sliced several different ways.

Faces of Slovenia and a history rundown. Faces of today's Slovenia and a poem highlight some landmark events.

Dates of note. An abbreviated timeline takes you backwards in time, from Slovenia's admission into the European Union in 2004 and its Presidency in 2008 to the Stone Age. Information at the top of the page gives you the big picture, such as empires. The bottom of the page spotlights people and points of interest.

Louis Adamič. An excerpt from American author Louis Adamic's *The Native's Return* follows.

Castles. Thirteen castle museums are briefly introduced. A look at the seventeenth century inhabitants of two castles some 50 miles apart reveals two vastly different lives.

Next comes a behind-the-scenes glimpse of a restoration in progress, namely the Mirna castle just a few miles from Baron Valvasor's castle.

The history section concludes with reflections on two individuals whose lives spanned regime changes and how they dealt with it.

A Few Basics

Ljubljana

Slovenia

- Size: almost 8,000 square miles (a bit bigger than New Jersey)
- Population: about 2,000,000 (about a 1/4 of New Jersey Probably half speak English, and increasingly so
- Currency: Euro
- Language: Slovenian, a Slavic language (Hungarian and Italian near those borders; English is the most common second language.)
- Capital: Ljubljana Population about 330,000 as of the year 2000 Maribor – 2nd largest, Celje – 3rd
- Bordering countries: Italy, Austria, Hungary, Croatia
- Mountain Ranges: Julian Alps, Karavanke Alps, Kamnik-Savinja Alps
- Highest Peak: Triglav, about 9,400 feet
- Largest Park: Triglav National Park with about 207,000 acres
- Largest Lake: Cerknica (intermittent) 10 square miles
- Longest river: Sava 137 miles
- Highest waterfall: Čedca, 426 feet

The Slovenian Flag

The images on Slovenia's flag refer to milestones on the way to independence. White, blue and red stripes come from the coat of arms of the Duchy of Carniola, from a time considered to be a period of fair rule and freedom beginning under Otto the Great in 955. This period inspired Slovenia's intellectuals during the 1848 "Springtime of Nations," when the idea of a separate country for South Slavs of the former Austrian Empire came into fruition.

On the shield in the upper left of the tri-color, Triglav Mountain's three white peaks sit above two waves, one for the Adriatic Sea and one for the rivers. Three golden stars honor the Žovnek Counts of Celje whose court became a European center in the fifteenth century.

The works of Slovenia's national poet France Prešeren and architect Jože Plečnik influenced the design. France Prešeren's poems praised the beauty of the Slovenian Alps and waterways. On the back of a statue completed by Jože Plečnik years before Slovenia's independence in 1991, he inscribed the symbol that was adopted, almost without change, as Slovenia's new flag.

Freedom's Flame, Long-Kindled

Slovenia, now land and nation,
Centuries sought this combination.
Mountains listened, rivers talked;
Time flowed toward its destination.

Past habitants, Illyrians
Lived back a few millennia.
Celts and Romans, Lombard, Hun,
Noric Kingdom, Byzantia.

From the East in late five hundreds,
Tribes of Slavs began migrations,
Came from forests near Carpathians,
Followed rivers' perambulations.

Seventh century Carantania
With King Samo drove back the Avars,
A Slavic state, sanctum sanctorum,
Frankish rule, marca Vinedorum.

Holy Romans, Empire Hapsburg
Serfdom, struggle, Slavic writing.
By seventeen hundreds Maria Theresa
Let Slovenians speak Slovenian.

Napoleon, in the nineteenth century,
Brought new hope for rule of law.
Back came Austrian feudalism,
And dimmed the light of coming dawn.

Pre-World War One the Spring of Nations
Bound Serbs, Slovenians, and Croatians.
Yugoslavia, pulled out from Ost Reich,
'Til '91 were South Slav nation.

Freedom flamed late twentieth century.
Thirteen hundred years it had glimmered.
Slovenia, jubilant, bright young nation
Your fire has led you each generation.

Some Historic Benchmarks of the Lands now Slovenia

In the Current Era:

2008 – *President of European Union*
2004 – *Member of European Union and United Nations*
1991 – *Declaration of Independence as Slovenian Nation*
1945 – *A Republic in the new Yugoslavia*
1941 – *Divided among Germany, Italy and Hungary*
1929 – *Kingdom of Yugoslavia*
1918 – *Kingdom of Serbs, Croats and Slovenians*
1867 – *Austro-Hungarian Empire*
1809 – *Illyrian Provinces*
1278 – *Hapsburg Empire*
820 – *Holy Roman Empire*
560 – *Empire of Carantania*
500 - *Slavic Migrations*
394 - *Byzantine Empire*

Before the Current Era:

100 – *Roman Settlements*
200–15 – *Noric Kingdom*
700–200 – *Hallstatt Period*

A Short Report of a Long History

Slovenia at the Crossroads

Where East meets West, and North joins South

The purpose of this timeline is to acquaint you with Slovenia's past and present inhabitants, now predominantly of Slavic heritage. Control of this globally strategic intersection has been an issue throughout history. The summary in the next few pages should give you a framework for better understanding the many historically significant monuments and documents in the country.

The timeline runs from present to past. The first page covers 15 years, the last page 60,000. The pages in-between average about 100 years each, depending on changes in population and government.

Information about ethnicity and rule is given at the top of the page. Maps, sketches and supporting data occupy the lower part of the page. Headings are intended for convenience only.

"Mladina." Young Freedom-Forging Forces

Slovenia's youth fanned flames for independence.
They wrapped messages in rock music, and
shouted out allegories against oppression.
Their steady drumbeat crescendoed into
an ultimatum for autonomy.

"Laibach," the German word for "Ljubljana," was the name of a Slovenian band that established itself internationally in the late 1980s. According to Mark Thompson, the London correspondent for the Mladina newspaper in those years, with "sledgehammer percussion, hunting horns, ranting lyrics and khaki uniforms, they looked and sounded like fascists." You didn't need to understand their words to feel the pulsating protest against militarism and totalitarianism.

Had the government clamped down too hard on expressive youth such as these, however, the tenuous federation of Yugoslavia could have imploded earlier than it did.

I chanced to be in Ljubljana on the day in 1988 that proved to be the breaking point. You could tell at once that the day belonged to history. The otherwise loquacious populace just listened. Every man, woman and child clutched a transistor or clustered near a radio. At a military court in Ljubljana on that day, four writers were on trial for articles they had published in the newspaper "Mladina," or "Youth." As I recall, they were accused of publicizing names of those the Yugoslav military intended to eliminate. Yugoslavia, consisting of the Republics of Serbia (biggest in population and land), Croatia, Slovenia, Montegro, Bosnia-Hercegovina, and Macedonia, operated under the Serb-dominated military.

"Mladina" had begun as a newspaper of the Communist Youth Organization but became an outspoken critic of governmental abuses. Like the radio station and rock bands in Ljubljana at the time, it operated on an almost clandestine basis, printing at various locations and generally trying to fly below the radar. "Mladina" grew to symbolize much more than either youth or politics.

Two issues about the trial riled people. The court was military instead of civil and the proceedings were conducted in the Serbo-Croatian language instead of Slovenian. As the four defendants were led away to prison after the trial, some 10,000 silent Slovenians stood near the courthouse and held flowers up to them.

The sentencing of the Mladina authors coalesced Slovenians against the government. Slovenia demanded greater autonomy in the Yugoslav government and continued to press even as its demand was rejected.

On June 25th, 1991, the Slovenian parliament declared independence.

The new Slovenian flag ran up flagpoles at border crossings. "REPUBLIKA SLOVENIJA." signs replaced "Socialistična Federativna Republika Jugoslavija." Slovenia braced for the repercussions of its defiant acts.

Buses and trucks were piled at roads into Slovenia from Croatia to slow the Yugoslav army's onslaught. Brnik Airport was hit with air strikes. Tanks rolled into the streets of Ljubljana. Demonstrations broke out in Innsbruck and Vienna to support Slovenia's efforts to break away from Yugoslavia. A busload of mothers headed to other parts of Yugoslavia in search of their captured soldiers.

Ten days and 18 deaths later, the tiny new country emerged intact. In terms of its value to Europe as a free, independent nation, Slovenia offered stability and a bridgehead to an otherwise divisive region. In the early 2000s Slovenia gained admission to NATO and the European Union.

Raising the flag at the proclamation of independence and sovereignty of the Republic of Slovenia, on June 25th 1991, at Trg Republike (Republic Square) in Ljubljana.

The Time Line with a View of the Past

2008	2004		1992	**1991**	1990

Yugoslavia

2008
Presidency of the European Union.

2004
Slovenia was accepted as a member of the European Community and the United Nations.

1992
Slovenia was recognized as an independent country by the European Union and the United Nations

June 25, 1991
Slovenia declared its sovereignty as an independent state.

1990
Slovenia declared independence following a plebescite vote.

1945
Slovenia became a republic in the new Yugoslavia.

The then Slovenian President Milan Kučan speaking at the meeting of the European Parliament in Brussels in 2001.

Danilo Türk (the President of the Republic of Slovenia since 2008), chairing the UN Security Council during the presidency of the Republic of Slovenia, New York, 1998.

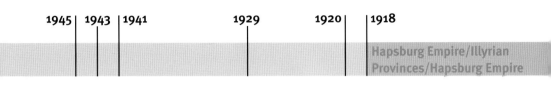

| 1945 | 1943 | 1941 | 1929 | 1920 | 1918 |

1943

Marshal Josip Broz Tito, of Slovenian and Croatian descent, was elected President of the National Committee of the Liberation of Yugoslavia and ruled until his death in 1980. Tito kept Yugoslavia positioned between East and West but beyond the grasp of either with a socialism that took some features from Russia's communistic system but added some western-style freedoms. For some 36 years he held together six republics with multiple religions, languages, and backgrounds.

1941

Slovenia was divided among Germany, Italy and Hungary.

1929

The Kingdom of Serbs, Croats and Slovenians changed into the Kingdom of Yugoslavia. Most of Slovenia fell under the designation of Dravska Banovina.

1920

Carinthia in large part joined Austria while a small part stayed with the Kingdom of Serbs, Croats and Slovenians following a Carinthian plebescite.

1918

Slovenia became part of the Kingdom of Serbs, Croats and Slovenians ending Austrian rule.

Leon Štukelj (1898–1999), Olympic champion, lawyer and judge, won gold medals in gymnastics in Paris in 1924, in Amsterdam in 1928. Born in Novo Mesto, he later moved to Lenart and then to Maribor. For almost a decade he claimed the distinction as the oldest living Olympic champion in the world and was presented at the opening ceremonies of the 1996 Olympiad in Atlanta. In 1997 he was inducted into the International Gymnastics Hall of Fame. All of Slovenia celebrated his 100th birthday in 1998, and a sports hall in Novo Mesto bears his name.

Leon Štukelj during his floor exercise at the Olympic Games in Berlin in 1936.

Hapsburg Empire/Illyrian Provinces/Hapsburg Empire

Springtime of Nations

1848

Austrian Emperor Ferdinand's Manifesto marked the end of the feudal system. Slovenes sought their own identity within the Hapsburg Empire, citing their Caranthanian history dating back to the 7th century.

1848 – 1918

Springtime of Nations, an era in which the notion of a united Slavic state blossomed among the Slavic populations then under Austrian rule

France Prešeren

Jože Plečnik

18th and 19th century Luminaries

France Prešeren (1800 – 1849) led the cause for Slovenian unity through his poetry, verse and writing.

Jože Plečnik (1872 – 1957) architect of Ljubljana's most notable features, designed Tromostovje (Three Bridges) the city's public market, university library, and cemetery.

Ivan Cankar (1876 – 1918) Slovenia's most esteemed writer defended the down-trodden and satirized those who exploited them.

Author Oton Župančič (1878 – 1949) heralded the importance of individual expression and of maintaining an affinity with other Slavic peoples.

Patron of the arts and poet **Baron Sigismund Zois** (1747 – 1819) founded the Zois literary circle.

Jurij Vega (1754 – 1802), mathematician, devised logarithm tables.

Baroque sculptor **Francesco Robba** (1698 – 1757) lived in Ljubljana.

1813
1814 **1809** **1782** **1774**

1814
Austrian rule and feudalism were reinstated by Metternich.

1809 – 1813
Carinthia, Carniola, Gorizia, Trieste, Istria and Dalmatia become part of Napoleon's Illyrian Provinces, with Ljubljana as the capital. The Slovenian language was encouraged, as well as French and Italian languages, local education and culture. The feudal system was replaced by the Code Napoléon, and war reparations were imposed.

1782
Serfs were freed, freedom of religion allowed and religious orders abolished by Emperor Josef II, reforms that were reversed on his deathbed.

1774
The Slovenian language was mandated to be used in education and elementary schools by imperial decree of the Austrian Empress Maria Theresa.

Coat of arms of the Philharmonic Academy from 1701.

Anton Tomaž Linhart

Beginnings
1701 – The Academia Philharmonicorum in Ljubljana became one of the first in Central Europe.
1789 – Anton Tomaž Linhart wrote the first **play** in the Slovenian language.
1797 – Poet and journalist Valentin Vodnik initiated the first **newspaper** in the Slovenian language.
1794 – The first **Philharmonic Society** in Central Europe was established in Ljubljana, with Beethoven, Paganini, and Brahms as honorary members. Joseph Haydn, first honorary, presented the Society with a score of his composition, in Tempore belli.

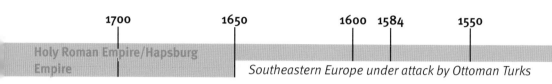

1700	1650	1600	1584	1550

Holy Roman Empire/Hapsburg Empire

Southeastern Europe under attack by Ottoman Turks

1600s
Counter-reformation

1408 – mid-1600s
Southeastern Europe was under attack by Ottoman Turks. In addition to paying tribute to the overlords, peasants had to provide for their own defense against invaders.

1400s
The Counts of Celje rose to prominence as European nobility in the 14th century.
Owning 20 castles within Slovenia and several outside through their daughters, they ushered in a time of native rule, opulence and humanistic thinking centered in Celje. When the last male was assassinated in 1456, holdings of the entire dynasty passed to their rival Hapsburgs.
Ulrich I of Celje, lord of Zovnek, who died in 1312, was the first Count of Celje.
Anna of Celje (1381-1416) became Queen of Poland and Lithuania.
Barbara of Celje (c. 1390/1395-1451) held the title of Holy Roman Empress.
Margaret of Celje, (d. 1480) heiress of the dynasty, married Count Herman of Montfort and later Duke Vladislav of Teschen.

Town of Celje

Kranj and Aquileia, two early major medieval towns.
At the end of the 10th century, the German ruling class made grants of Slovenia's lands to religious and secular lords, beginning two centuries of Germanization. Landholders included the archbishops of Salzburg, Aquileian patriarchs, bishops of Freising and Brixen, families of Eppsteins, Spanheims, Andechs-Meran, and Counts of Bogen, Carinthia and Gorizia.

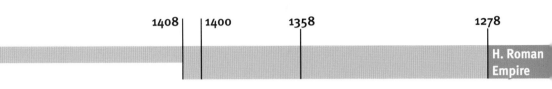
1278
Slovenia became part of the dynasty which was founded by Rudolf Hapsburg lasted until 1918. Styria, Carinthia and Carniola were given to Rudolf's sons and relatives in 1282.

Freising Documents, the oldest preserved Slovenian texts, originated in Upper Carinthia, near today's Austrian Moll Valley or Lurnfeld, between 972 and 1039 C.E.

Primož Trubar

Jacobus Gallus Carniolus

From 1358–1848
More than 100 peasant uprisings and revolts occurred, reaching their peak between 1478 and 1573. At issue were the tributes required by the feudal lords and the democratic election of priests. At least one attempt was made to form a peasant state under the control of the Emperor, and in at least one instance Slovenians and Croatians combined forces, pulled down castles and executed overlords.

At the end of the first millennium, the standard of living of people under the Carolingian rulers of the Holy Roman Empire was only about one tenth of what it had been under the Roman emperors.

Hapsburg rulers simultaneously took the titles of King of Bohemia and Hungary, Archduke of Austria, Duke of Styria, Count of Tyrol, and Lord of Trieste.

Primož Trubar (1508–1586), author of the first text in Slovenian in 1550 and translator of the entire Bible into Slovenian in 1584, brought written native language to Slovenia.

Jacobus Gallus Carniolus (1550-1591) was a renowned Renaisaance composer.

Baron Janez Vajkard Valvasor (1641-1693) wrote, illustrated and published the first and still definitive work on the history and culture of Slovenia.

976

The Duchy of Greater Carantania was reinstated when Emperor Otto II gave the southwestern territories to Margrave Leopold, beginning a 270-year Babenberg rule.

955

Carantanians joined the Bavarians under Otto the Great to fight the Magyars and reconstituted the Ostmark. Carniola (Kranjska), Carinthia (Koroška), Styria (Štajerska), Gorizia (Goriška) and the White March (Bela Krajina) were formed by dividing up Carantania.

Early 900s

Lands were conquered and occupied by Magyars; the Ostmark disintegrated.

869 to 874

Carantanian Prince Kocelj established an independent realm in Lower Pannonia.

820 – 828

Carantania was reorganized as a Frankish border county or march and placed under the rule of Bavarian dukes

791 – 799

Charlemagne campaigned against the Avars. Literacy was encouraged in 863 when the brothers Cyril and Methodius brought Slavic language translations of the Bible to southeastern Europe.

The Frankish empire expanded and learning flourished after Charlemagne was crowned as Emperor of the Holy Roman Empire in 800. Feudalism spread, richly rewarding the nobility with landholdings.

Knežji Kamen – The Duke's Stone

An old democratic tradition appears to have been practised by Slovenia's forbears as early as 611. Carantanians, and later Carinthians, gathered around the Duke's Stone in the middle of a field, questioned their dukes and ended with a slap to symbolize the public's right to object. Each duke had to take a seat on the leader's chair and swear an oath. The people would then accept them as rulers.

These proceedings were conducted in the Slovenian language and until 1414 were held in the fields of Gospasveta near Celovec, now Maria Saal near Klagenfurt in southern Austria. Thereafter, the ritual was moved to the Ducal Throne and continued in the State House of Klagenfurt until 1728, when Institutio Sclavenica was made part of the Austrian Constitution. The sixteenth century French jurist Jean Bodin mentioned this ritual in his writings on republics. In 1999, U.S. President Clinton said in a state visit to Slovenia:

"You see, Thomas Jefferson loved the fact that before assuming their titles, the old dukes of Carinthia were ceremoniously slapped by a local peasant to symbolize the right of the people to rebuff their leaders. Thomas Jefferson liked that. So did all future generations of Americans. Except they wait until after you're in office to do it.

"Župan" and "knez" meant "chief" initially, but later connoted aristocratic positions such as "duke" or "prince." "Vojvoda" meant "head of a military command" early on, but later changed to denote a governor.

700
Slavs were subjugated as serfs by colonizing Bavarians.

630
Prince Valuk led the Principality of Slavs in the eastern Alps.

628
Alpine Slavs defeated the Bavarii near Aguntum, now in Austria's Tyrol.

"I hail from Styria." / "I'm a Carinthian."

Residents of the Austrian province of Steiermark and Slovenian Stajerska still tend to identify themselves as Styrians first, just as people from Karnten in Austria or Koroska in Slovenia think of themselves as Carinthians above all.

The roots of such strong territorial loyalty in these two provinces reach all the way back to the time when Otto the Great first reconstituted the Ostmark in 955, dividing Carantania into Carniola (Kranjska), Carinthia (Koroska), Stryia (Stajerska), Gorizia (Goriska), and the White March known as Bela Krajina. The tribal system of 7th century Carantania had begun falling to feudalism in the early Middle Ages, around a hundred years after the Slavs had joined the Frankish Samo to form the kingdom of Carantania. Eighth century Carolingians, twelfth century Babenburg Princes, and thirteenth century Hapsburgs successively tightened the grip of serfdom on their Slavic subjects.

Up until the 19th century, the areas of Styria and Carinthia, along with Austria's Vorarlberg and Tyrol, were known as Länder in the Austrian empire.

Each area possessed a strong attachment to the home-territory, jealously guarded their autonomy and resisted efforts to join a nation-state, the popular political notion of the times. Whereas the northern bounds of the Austrian Empire modeled themselves after Vienna, the southerners held tightly to their own heritage.

Also known as the Estates, Austria's southern districts furnished both advisers and military strength for nobles who ruled them. In the late Middle Ages they paid tribute directly to the monarch instead of going through normal administrative channels. Even despite Hapsburg absolutist rule, the Länder maintained their original form to a large extent. They kept their capital cities, their heraldry, folk costumes and legends. In 1918 when the Hapsburg monarchy collapsed, the Lander guarded their positions as distinct parts of the new Austrian republic.

Today, the Länder still claim their Landtage, or provincial seats of government, with separate flags, heraldry, and anthems. Dialects and dress also distinguish them, as well as independence in dealing with neighboring countries in regional affairs. Even though a part of modern Austria, Klagenfurt continues as the capital of Carinthia (Karnten), and Graz as the capital of Styria (Steiermark).

493
500
488

Migration of Alpine Slavs / Carantania

The Byzantine Empire – 1000
Years of Eastern Rule

500s

Slavs began settling along the Danube, Sava and Drava Rivers as they migrated, perhaps from the Carpathian Basin. Known as a peaceable people, they lived in forests along rivers and lakes, farming and breeding cattle. Socially they made no class distinctions. In perilous times they elected a leader, or "zupan." Initially called "Sclavi" or "Sclaveni" like other Slavs, they were referred to as "Slovenici" for the first time in the late 18th century.

Germanic tribes of Lombards, or Langobards (long beards) probably coming from southern Sweden, ended up in Italy. In 547 the Byzantine Emperor Justinian allowed them to settle in Pannonia and Noricum and in 568 they invaded northern Italy, still known today as Lombardia. By the 7th century Slavs had settled in areas abandoned by the Lombards.

King Samo's Carantania

Frankish weapon's merchant Samo led the Slavs in a successful revolt against the Avars, tribes from the East, who had subjugated the Slavs east of the Carpathian Mountains around 560 C.E. Once the Avars met defeat at Constantinople in the early 600s, Samo helped the Slavs allay the Avar threat at first in Moravia and Bohemia, and then in Central Europe.

Carantanians, as the Slavs occupying the large area north of the Karavanke Mountains were known, joined Samo's realm as the duchy of Marca Vinedorum. The first stable Slavic state of Carantania included parts of what is now the Czech Republic, Slovakia, Lower Austria and Slovenia. After Samo's death in 658 or 659, the empire largely dissolved, but the Slavic state of Carantania has continued in some form to the present.

The Carantanian Duke Ulric I's sister Mathilda was married to Theobold II. Their daughter Alice became Queen of France and mother of Philip II Augustus, King of France.

Enthronement of the Duke of Carinthia

493
Ostrogoth – or East Goth – leader Theodoric the Great ruled what is now Italy and Slovenia. Coins from that era have been found in Rifnik, Kranj, and near Kobarid.

488
Slavs and Avars began moving into the area following the Roman withdrawal.

400s
Roman provinces fell to Germanic tribal assaults.
Huns decimated Poetovio (Ptuj), Celeia (Celje) and Emona (Ljubljana).

394
The Byzantine Emperor Theodosius from Constantinople defeated Rome's Emperor Eugenius near Ajdovščina, now in Slovenia. The union of the Eastern and Western Holy Roman Empire lasted only until Theodosius' death the following year.

379
Visigoths – or West Goths - a Germanic tribe probably originating in southern Sweden, sacked Poetovio (now Ptuj). Various invading tribes moved across the corridor through Emona (Ljubljana) to reach Italy.

260
Huns, nomadic tribes from the Asian Steppes, entered Pannonia and swelled their armies with Germanic tribes from the Danube region.

The tomb of Enija at Šempeter in the Savinjska valley

Byzantium
Rome fell in 394, but the Holy Roman Empire flourished in the East for almost another thousand years as Byzantium. Its center shifted from Rome to Constantinople. The Holy Roman Empire ended in 1453 with the conquest of Constantinople.
Communication and trade from Constantinople emanated deep into Europe and Asia for more than a thousand years. Under Justinian's rule in the 6th century, Byzantium's borders stretched from Spain to Mesopotamia, from the Danube and the Black Sea to Africa's Mediterranean coast.
The Byzantine Empire preserved Greek thought and furthered art, architecture and science. The advancement of law under Justinian served as a future model for European law in easing the freedom of slaves, transfer of land, and inheritance of property.
Constantinople was sacked by the 4th Crusade in 1204. The Empire ended when Turkish rule began.

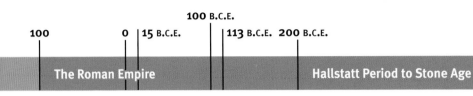

100 B.C.E.

| 100 | 0 | **15** B.C.E. | **113** B.C.E. | **200** B.C.E. |

The Roman Empire | **Hallstatt Period to Stone Age**

100–0
Romans settled in Slovenia at Emona (Ljubljana), Celeia (Celje), Poetovio (Ptuj), and Virunum (near Celovec in Slovenian, or Klagenfurt in German).

15 B.C.E.
The Noric Kingdom became part of Rome. The Norici gained Roman citizenship but kept their own elected officials, called doyens.
Celts entered Slovenia from the north in about 400 – 200 B.C.E., probably coming from Indo-Europe or the British Isles. Iron Age artifacts all across Europe attest to a wide-reaching influx.
Their three-class system was divided into warrior aristocracy, intellectuals (including druids, poets, and jurists), and everyone else. Celtic warriors terrified their enemies by running naked into battle, screaming and beating their swords on their shields. Women were leaders and participated in warfare.

113 B.C.E.
Taurisis, Celts of the Noric Kingdom that occupied the area now in central Slovenia, were defeated by the Cimbri and other Germanic tribes.

100–200 B.C.E.
Romans annexed the Noric Kingdom and divided it into *Noricum* (now Carinthia and western Styria) and *Upper* and *Lower Pannonia* (now eastern Styria much of Carniola, Primorska and Istria, which is now Croatia).
Noricum and Pannonia grew increasingly important to Rome for fending off invaders before they could reach Italy. Germanic tribes broke through the Roman fortifications known as "the Limes" by using Roman-built roads.
The Julian Alps were named after Julius Caesar following his visit there.

102 and 101 B.C.E.
Roman victories over Germanic tribes brought a peaceful period to the border state of Noricum. Mining and metalworking industries flourished, with silver coins minted at Celeia (today's Celje) and Noric steel swords acclaimed throughout the Roman Empire.

200 B.C.E.
The Noric Kingdom (the first Celtic kingdom in Europe) consisted of the strongest Celtic tribe Norici, Ljubljana marsh -dwelling Illyrians and about 11 other tribes in the region that is now Slovenia and southern Austria.

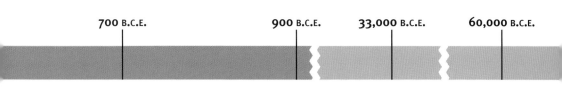

700 B.C.E.

Hallstatt Period iron helmets, gold jewelry and embossed vessels have been found in Stična and Vače from around the fifth century B.C.E. after Indo-European Illyrian tribes invaded the Ljubljana marsh dwellers from the south and inhabited the valley of the Upper Sava River.

900–200 B.C.E.

Bronze Age marsh dwellers farmed and raised cattle near Ljubljana and Cerknica, and traded with Italy, northern Europe and the Balkans via the "Amber Route," which experts believe to have crossed through present-day Ljubljana.

33,000 B.C.E.

A Stone Age bone flute, the first known musical instrument, has been found near Cerknica.

60,000 B.C.E.

Stone Age tools of bone and stone have been found in a cave in Upper Savinja Valley's Mt. Olševa.

Vače situla (bronze silver-plated pail)

The Native's Return

From the story of Louis Adamic's return to Yugoslavia in 1932, after leaving in 1913 and then serving in the US army.

"The short train ride from Trieste to Ljubljana was a delightful experience, especially after we crossed the Italian border, when I was in my old country at last.

It was a perfect midspring afternoon, and most of my misgivings of the week before had vanished. Carniola, to all seeming, had not changed a whit. Here was the same river Sava with the same tributaries; the same little lakes and waterfalls; the same thickly wooded hills and mountains, with the snow-capped peaks above them; the same fields and meadows; the same villages and little churches, with crude frescoes of saints painted by peasant artists on the outer walls; and the same people, tilling in the same old way – slowly, patiently, somewhat inefficiently (to my American eyes) with semi-primitive tools and implements, on the same fertile black soil. The World War (although some of the worst battles were fought within hearing distance from Carniola) and the drastic political change, in 1918, from Austria to Yugoslavia had had no effect upon its essential aspects, its exquisite and wholesome beauty."

. . .

"I do not mean to say that the regions of Carniola by themselves, with all their congestion of lovely valleys, lakes, rivers, hills, woods and mountains, are more beautiful than other regions I have seen elsewhere in the world. I know of vastly grander places in the United States, but houses and towns in America, a new country, often spoil a natural scene. If not houses and towns, then outdoor advertisements and heaps of tin cans and discarded machinery. In Carniola, however, the simple peasant architecture of the small villages seems to enhance the beauty of the countryside. The houses and villages *belong*. They appear to have grown out of the soil. They belong exactly where they are, both aesthetically and economically. Most of them have been where they are for five, six, seven hundred years. They are harmonious with the woods, the fields, the lakes. They are in the pattern of the country as a whole, an elemental and sympathetic feature thereof."

...

"Young women, for instance, who die shortly before they are supposed to marry, become villé, or nymphs, and as such live for years – in the belief of some, forever - in the woods and fields, or by the streams, lakes or waterfalls near the villages. These nymphs, as a rule, are beautiful, benevolent spirits. Once upon a time, when the world was a much better place than it is today, they lived in close contact and friendship with human beings still in the flesh. In those days they regularly helped peasants at their work. At night people saw them in the fields, pulling out weeds and cockles; or in the meadows, dancing and chanting, urging the grass to grow tall and thick, so the good peasants would have plenty of hay for their stock in the wintertime. When shepherds fell asleep, the nymphs watched their sheep and cattle."

...

"The old man's death meant simply that he was being transferred from their care to the care of the beautiful nymph, who is a creature of their pagan imaginations, slightly overlaid with a dressing of Christian thought and practice. . . .These explanations and beliefs are the result of the people's long background, reaching back into the pagan era and their background, in its essence, . . This whole village appears to be in deep harmony with the region. It is an indigenous part of it. And these people belong here as much as these swallows flying about. They are intimate with their surroundings. They know what their function is without ever really thinking about it. Death is only a part, an inevitable incident, in that intimacy with their environment; and, like other incidents in their lives, they have glossed it over with poetry and semi-religious beliefs. . . ".

An American Immigrant Visits Yugoslavia and Discovers His Old Country, by Louis Adamic. Fully illustrated, Harper & Sons, New York & London, 1934.

Person, Place and Politics

Maybe it comes from centuries of being at the crossroads, but Slovenians seem to have a unique ability to separate the individual from the political regime. Two instances were particularly striking to me.

One involves the father of friends in Graz. The first time I met this wonderful, gracious gentleman, he thanked me personally as a way of expressing his immense gratitude to the Slovenian people. The story he then told held us spellbound.

During World War II he had been a German soldier and found himself stranded in the Alps near Bled. A farm family hid him in their stable, brought him food and clothing for many months, and eventually helped him to escape back over the Alps into Austria when the time was right.

After the war, the Austrian soldier went back to the small village, located that family and said he wanted to make a gift to them – whatever they chose – in return for the kindness they had shown him during the war. The father of the family took him upstairs into the loft of the farmhouse and showed him a large room that he had made into a library filled with books. The thing he wanted most, the farmer said, was a bust of Goethe for the library.

The two families continue their friendship across the borders. A few years ago after a fire had destroyed their home, the Slovenians even temporarily moved up into a Graz apartment that belonged to their friends. Rebuilding the library, no doubt, took top priority as a joint effort.

The second story is probably the same story of thousands of people who were relocated in the 1940s and even 50s. I have heard specifics only once, although I spent many hours with my relatives in the little hilltop village of Dole throughout the years.

Sometimes my visits coincided with my relatives' German friends who came to stay for two weeks at the *gostilna* (inn) each summer. They were always introduced by Pavla as longtime friends she had made when they lived in Germany. Other *gostilna* guests brought out their German and spoke to the best of their varying abilities.

The one time that I heard the details about how Pavla went to Germany occurred when Pavla (pronounced 'Powell-a'), my father's cousin's wife, traveled with my two children and me south into Serbia. On the way to reach the main road, we passed the town where she and others from the hills around Dole had been herded into railroad cars and hauled to Mannheim, Germany. She must have been about 18 at the time.

In Germany, Pavla worked in a factory for a number of years before she was allowed to come home once the war had ended. During that time she had made friends with the family that then came back year after year to stay with them in Dole, walk the hills, take the baths, help out in the kitchen and greet the gostilna regulars. The discussion revolved around how things had changed in Germany, since many others had been relocated too and were anxious to hear news. Politics were always openly discussed, but from the perspective that everyone lived the same history one way or another, but without being responsible for it.

Pavla's husband Tone had been relocated to Graz and also maintained ties there after the war. He often made buying trips there for the gostilna, conducting business with contacts he had made while living there. During the war Pavla and Tone had been separated for a number of years by the relocations. Once they returned to Dole, they married and took over the gostilna that had come up for sale.

Before and during the war, the hills around Dole had been a stronghold of the Partisans, Marshal Josip Broz Tito's base group. The thick-walled house on the ridge where my grandmother was born had been a Partisan stronghold, was burned by the German soldiers and used as their base, since you can see for miles in all directions from that vantage point. After the war the house had been rebuilt and now operates as a gostilna and farm by other descendants of my grandmother, cousins of the Dole gostilna owners.

From our very first visit to Dole and the gostilna in 1967, I marveled at the people who would make their way there, from Sarajevo, Austria, Italy, England, Switzerland. As then, history continues to be a prominent subject of group discussions and current events hold the limelight, but personal lives captivate everyone's attention.

Land of 100 castles

Look inside Slovenia's restored aristocratic residences for insights into the past. Regional displays give a feel for the surrounding areas, past and present. Gardens, boutiques and cafés may provide local specialties and information. Check Slovenia's official website *www.slovenia-tourism.si* for castles with new offerings of lodging.

Estates that have been converted to resort complexes usually welcome day guests to their restaurants and grounds.

The old pharmacy in the Olimje monastery

Come to the Castles

Step back in time
To a much different age
When nobles in castles
Took charge of the stage.

They dressed in great armor
And mustered a group,
Set off on horseback,
Defended their troop.

Now you can enter
Where empires held sway,
Look at the bounty
And maps of their day.

Stroll in their gardens;
Have tea in their rooms.
Breathe in the air
Of the new flower that blooms.

< Mokrice castle

The city of Ljubljana

Ljubljana, Roman Emona, Medieval Laibach

Ljubljana's premiere castle, first mentioned as Laibach in 1144, still goes by the Romanized Celtic term for "round-walled hilltop fortification," the *castrum capitalis.* Some earliest known inhabitants bore names like Gregor, Wodolricus, Rodolfus, Adelbertus, Marquardus, Arnoldus, Putzlinus, Ysenricus, Gyselbertus, Raiwigus, Weizmannus, Hamelricus, Wariendo. In the mid-1100s the castle was used by Dukes Bernard and Spanheim to mint coins.

At Spanheim's death, the fortress passed to the Bohemian king Otokar, and in 1278 to Rudolf Hapsburg, head of the Holy Roman Empire, who then sold it to an earl from the Gorica-Tyrol region.

The fortress, completely destroyed in the 1511 earthquake, was rebuilt in the mid-16th century and repaired after the 1895 earthquake.

Today a footpath from Ljubljana's old town leads up to the castle museum park. The old core of the fort has been preserved, some interiors restored to the 15th century condition, and a café and gift shop added. Many art and music events take place in the castle grounds.

Bled castle

Bled, Early Resort Destination, Castellum Veldes

With roots dating back to the 11th century, the present-day castle perches 125 meters up on the sheer rock cliffs above Lake Bled. In 1004, after the Holy Roman Emperor Henrik II gave the property to the Catholic Bishops, it grew into a stronghold for literacy and culture.

From the earliest recorded history, the beauty of Lake Bled has drawn travelers and residents. Postcard-perfect against a backdrop of alpine splendor, the turreted fortress reflects in the still waters, ringed by high stone walls. This pristine setting is jealously guarded against modern development. As you walk around the water's edge or take an old-fashioned boat out to the picturesque island, your view will be essentially the same as it has been for the past several centuries.

Bled lies about 30 miles northeast of Ljubljana, about 15 miles beyond Kranj.

The town of Kranj

Kranj of Carniola, 10th century tombs and Renaissance halls.

Although not recently used as a castle, the upper stories of Kranj's city hall date back to the 1500s and its museum guards many past treasures. As part of ancient Carantania, a piece of which became Carniola in 955, the city of Kranj has managed to keep its medieval design more or less intact during its continuous role in the regional past.

Informational placards will lead you through stone and bronze-age history evidenced by artifacts found nearby. You can look back into 10th century subterranean crypts through glass floors and observe 16th century Renaissance style upstairs in ornately carved wooden chambers. You will also see a colorful collection of wooden chests, once used both for seating and storage.

A quick trip on the toll road, head northwest from Ljubljana for about 15 miles.

Kapucin bridge, Škofja Loka from 1892

Škofja Loka, view towards Loka castle

Škofja Loka, castrum Loka

In 973 under the Holy Roman Emperor Oton II, and later as home of the Freising lords until the early 1800s, Škofja Loka's castle now contains a museum of ethnological and archeological significance.

Parting the fields of wildflowers, a pathway leads up the hill from Škofja Loka's old town to a stately domed tower.

With a commanding view of the surrounding hills and valleys, the former residence of dukes and princes doubles as a wedding palace for the locals. Tucked underneath the main building, in the former dungeon, a well-appointed pub keeps its guests cool and happier than former occupants.

Škofja Loka is located about 14 miles northwest of Ljubljana.

Predjama castle

Predjama, Luegg Seat of the Earls of Goriške.

Each summer, a medieval festival replays memories of a legendary old robber baron who kept the emperors in Vienna busy for years trying to annihilate him. Slipping through secret passageways in steep rocky cliffs, Erazem Predjamski is reputed to have thrown cherries at his would-be capturers to further their frustration. He held out until 1484, after which the castle was occupied by a succession of nobles.

During festival time you can retrace the route of Erazem's many escapes. Allow time also to enjoy the scenery from the café terrace.

Go through Postojna to reach Predjama, about 30 miles southwest of Ljubljana. Predjama will be another 12 miles or so on small roads.

Piran

Piran, Greek "fire", Roman "Piranum"

Although only the surrounding walls now remain from the high castle on the bluff, crenelated ramparts and towers give the feel of its former grandeur.

The quaint harbor town of Piran bears its fiery name from Greek times but the terracotta look comes from its days under Venetian sway. A cobbled stone street leads to the castle gates overlooking both the town of Piran and the miles of Adriatic coastline. Some 600 feet of the original city wall still remain intact.

The whole town of Piran guards its historical landmark designation, so plan to take a bus or arrive very early to get a place in the small parking lot at the town's entry.

You will find Piran about 75 miles southwest of Ljubljana, mostly on the toll road.

The old castle above Celje

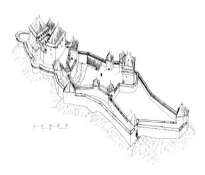

Celje, 15th Century European Splendor

Two castles in the former Roman settlement of Celeia are well worth a visit. Both date from the 1400s when Celje's Žovnek counts rose to power by intermarriage among the aristocratic families of Europe. The fortress above Celje looks over the rolling hills of the Sava River Valley, while the newer city residence sits midway between the primary downtown pedestrian-street and wide flood plains. Be sure to look up at the coffered, decorated ceiling in the downtown dwelling. The museum there also displays an impressive number of artifacts dating from all the way back to the Stone Age, detailing locations of discovery and eras to which they belong.

Celje was known by the Celts as Keleia, but the Romans changed the name to Celeia and expanded the settlement.

Find Celje about halfway to Maribor from Ljubljana, an easy 50 miles northeast on the toll road.

The oldest vine in Slovenia in Lent, Maribor

Maribor, Slovenia's leading Styrian city

Part of the old Carantania that was divided into Carinthia, Carniola and Styria in 955, Maribor now serves as the capital of the Slovenian part of Styria. Well-situated on the river Drava, the town had become known as a market town and as a wine producer by the 15th century.

The Baroque castle in today's downtown houses a festival hall and regional museum. Items of interest include Jewish grave markers from the 1300s, glass and ironworks, a clock and other items relating to Maribor's history as a guild and crafts center.

Maribor is located just south of the Austrian border, about 75 miles northeast of Ljubljana on the toll road.

The wine cellars, Ptuj

Ptuj, Slovenia's oldest Roman Settlement site, Poetovio

Overlooking a wide plain to the vineyard-strewn hills of Haloze, the Roman city of Poetovio perched at the edge of the old Roman marches, the first line of defense against invaders. As a result of its prime position, the fortress saw continual assault coming from the east, and the many rebuilding efforts that followed. Glass beads made here by the Romans form a permanent part of the castle museum's display and have been found in the far reaches of Western Europe. Ancient paintings on glass also originated here.

From Ljubljana, head northwest on the toll road for about 65 miles, and exit at Slovenska Bistrica. Take a smaller road east for about 20 miles.

Murska Sobota castle

Murska Sobota, Renaissance Manor in Prekmurje

On the Pannonian plains, in Slovenia's farthest eastern region of Prekmurje, you will find the castle surrounded by extensive parklands just west of the town of Murska Sobota. Artifacts in the museum relate to the history of the lands under attack from tribes from the east. Exhibits also show the past importance of pottery and textile production.

In the late 1300s the Szechy family-owners of the property contributed to the art that is still apparent today in both the neighboring town of Lendava and Murska Sobota.

A restaurant occupies a corner off the courtyard at the lower level.

To reach Murska Sobota, go 75 miles northeast of Ljubljana on the toll road. About 5 miles north of Maribor follow the road east and northeast for about another 40 miles.

Bogenšperk castle

Bogenšperk. Wagensperg for Boltežar Wagen

While probably dating back to the 15th century, the residence is most esteemed for the twenty years of the 17th century that it was occupied by Baron Janez Vajkard Valvasor. During that time, the author, publisher, artist and cartographer produced his monumental tomes, *The Glories of the Duchy of Carniola*. Still the definitive work on the society and people of the times, Baron Valvasor's descriptions painted lively accounts of life in the region, both with line drawings and narrative accounts.

Take the road to Litija about 5 miles northeast of Ljubljana and follow the river Sava east until you cross it in the town of Litija. Head south for about 5 miles through the village of Šmartno and watch for signs to lead you southeast to Bogenšperk.

Metlika castle

Metlika, Möttling

The fortress at Metlika was first mentioned in 1338 and now lies in the heart of Bela Krajina, or the White March. Some writings about the "Metling" area at the beginning of the 1300's tell of a new market settlement there. A few years later, the fort property was awarded by the Holy Roman minister Hmeljiniške to an earl named Henrik, who then built a single-story structure. Early occupants included Niklein Hmeljniški, Nikolaj Plesell, Seifried Gallenberg, Hans Hohenwarter and Jurij Kolenc.

The castle museum contains Roman memorabilia found nearby from the first and second centuries, including grave markers and statues.

In the small park near the castle entrance, note the bust of Marshall Broz Tito, ruler of the former Yugoslavia and still considered a hero in many parts of the country.

To get to Metlika, take the road to Novo Mesto and after an approximately 40-mile trip to Novo Mesto, continue southeast for about 20 miles to Metlika.

Ribnica castle

Ribnica, Reiffnitz

The bastion at Ribnica was first referenced in 1263 as *castrum Reiuenz*. In 1040, the property was given by the Holy Roman Emperor Henrik III to a charcoal producer named Pilgrim as a part of the area around Cerknica, about 20 miles northwest. The building was mentioned in 1220 as Rewenicz, and in the 1400s as Reiffnitz, Reyffnicz and Reyffnycz.

In the middle of a small town known for its basketry, the castle is only a few steps from the main street. A double-leveled arcade now looks over flower gardens and a small stream.

You will find Ribnica about 30 miles southeast of Ljubljana on the road to Kočevje. A smaller "Ribnica" lies further west.

Life in Two Castles, a 17th Century Look

You may be surprised to know about the two inhabitants of **Bogenšperk** and **Ptuj** castles four centuries ago. Their two 17th century stories cover startling distances and ranges of activities.

Although the two homes were situated a relatively short distance from each other, the two men's experiences could scarcely be more different. A German-speaking man of Italian descent lived in Bogenšperk castle near Litija, about an hour's drive east from Ljubljana. A man of Hungarian extraction from Scotland owned the castle at Ptuj, on the top of the hill overlooking the Drava River just east of Maribor.

The Baron of Bogenšperk, Janez Vajkard **Valvasor,** produced the masterpiece *"The Glories of the Dutchy of Carniola,"* a remarkable report of life and land in the 1600s. Traveling on horseback with a servant and a dog in today's northern Slovenia and southern Austria, the Baron sketched, mapped and described the lives of people in the countryside

The town of Ptuj

and cities. Today his work continues to be held in high regard as the most comprehensive account of that period.

In addition to copperplate maps and castle renderings, the book gives a colorful account of the times. For example, Baron Valvasor expressed astonishment at the locals around his Bogenšperk castle. While he found them to be congenial and marveled at their hardiness, he noted with surprise that they even walked around with their chests bared in the dead of winter!

During his travels, the Baron made particular note of natural phenomena and attempted to explain the unseen forces responsible for them, particularly caves and disappearing streams in the karst regions. His theory of interconnecting underground pools for the intermittently disappearing lake at Cerknica won him a position in the English Royal Society.

About 90 kilometers northeast of Baron Valvasor's castle, Walter Leslie of Scotland held sway at Ptuj. Part of the Leslie family had come from Hungary to Scotland in the 11th century. Walter's ancestor Bartholomew arrived in the Isles with the early English king Edmund Ironside's Hungarian decendant Margaret who then married Malcolm III, later the King of Scots. Bartholomew Leslie, knighted Lord Leslie, became the governor of Edinburgh Castle and held lands in Fife, the Mearns and Aberdeenshire.

Several centuries later, Walter Leslie left England, aligned himself with the Austrian king Ferdinand II, and led an assassination plot against the king's rival, General Albrecht Wallenstein. In return he became Imperial Chamberlain, received a grand estate in Bohemia, became the Count of the Holy Roman Empire, served as emissary to foreign lands and married the daughter of the Dietrichstein Prince Maximillian.

Having no children of his own, Walter Leslie groomed his nephew for the eventual inheritance of his lands in the Ostmark. The young James Leslie studied in Graz in today's southern Austria, where his uncle Walter also acquired substantial land holdings. According to some reports, James accompanied his uncle to Constantinople to negotiate a peace treaty with the Turks and married Maria Aloysia of Liechtenstein in 1666 shortly after he returned. One year later Walter died at the age of 61 and was buried in the Benedictine Abbey of the Scots (Schottenkirche) in Vienna under the combined Leslie-Dietrichstein coat-of-arms.

The castles at both Ptuj and Bogenšperk are now open to the public and offer historical information on site. The

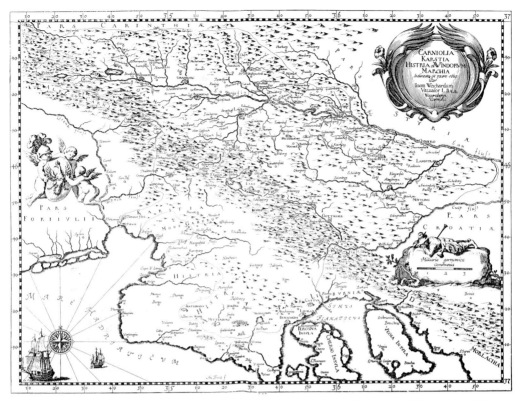

A map from 1689, the glory of Duchy of Carniola
Janez Vajkard Valvasor

1994 Slovenian translation of Janez Valvasor's 16th century book, "Slava Vojvodine Kranjske," complete with maps and drawings, was published by Mladinska knjiga in Ljubljana. A 2002 book in Slovenian about the Leslie family at the Ptuj castle was published by the Pokrajinski muzej in Ptuj.

A Wealth of Natural Treasures

As you may have surmised from the castle settings, this is a country enamored with nature. Take the fascination with falling water, for instance. Not only does each of the 88 waterfalls have its own name, but an entire book is devoted to sketches, locations and particulars of each one of them.

Geologist's guided tour. To grasp the abundant natural riches here, this section gains the benefit of a geologist's eye. John Weber has studied Slovenian lands and taught at the university in Ljubljana. For him the landscape reveals hidden secrets about formation, which he shares with us in a number of especially dramatic cases.

Telltale Landscapes. Following his discussion is a look at a dozen vantage points where you can see beyond scenic landscapes and discern their geologic past.

Abundant parklands. This section identifies a few of Slovenia's parks for you, some of which contain Telltale Landscape vantage points. Many parks are already established and more are in the planning stage. You can choose between parks complete with trails, rangers and amenities and those marked for the future but without services.

Thermal baths. Here you will find ancient indulgences with great wellness benefits - hot springs health resorts. These centers combine active recreation and quiet enjoyment in the tradition of the Roman baths. User-friendly for all ages and abilities, they serve equally as places where teenagers congregate on dates and where grandparents play with their little ones. Walls of windows bring the outdoors inside, and some of the pools even merge indoor and outdoor spaces. Clean, well lighted and spacious, they provide electronic pass and locker systems for easy accessibility. You can drop in for a few hours, or stay for a week. For those worried about communication, a few typical signs are included to familiarize you with some ground rules.

Geology - lively and exciting

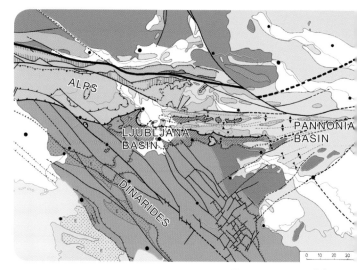

Tectonic structure of Slovenia

A Geologist's Puzzle

How do you crack
Earth's secret codes,
Buried deep in gran-
deur?

Divide by relief
four macroregions:
Alpine,
Mediterranean,
Dinaric and
Pannonian.

Categorize by climate
Continental,
Alpine and
Mediterrranean.

Parcel into
Macro-
Meso-
and Microregions.

View as a whole
vast, visible clues.
Examine the intricacy,
the composition, the
variation.

Study, tend,
catalog and measure
the Gargantuan Mystery
garden.

Ljubljana Basin - Classic Slovenia

The landscapes around Slovenia's capital city of Ljubljana and along the river Sava in central Slovenia provide the classic look of the country. Here you will find a mix of low flat valleys associated with young sediment and occasional tree-covered hills made up of ancient rock.

The low-lying region near Ljubljana known as the Ljubljana Basin belongs to a larger sedimentary basin called the Kranj Basin, both of which are probably actively sinking today. Both basins are filled with a thick layer of sediment that has been shed from the Alps and deposited by the river Sava and its tributaries. A few kilometers south of Ljubljana is the lowest part of the Ljubljana Basin, the Ljubljana Marshlands.

The interspersed individual tree-covered hills, such as Šmarna Gora, Homec Hill, Rožnik Hill in Tivoli Park, Golovec and Rudnik Hill, are former mountaintops that are now mostly sunken and buried by basin fill. One of the best places to see the older Paleozoic rocks is beneath the castle in Ljubljana.

The river Sava enters a deep gorge as it leaves the Kranj and Ljubljana Basins and begins cutting through one of Slovenia's most interesting geologic regions, the Sava Folds. This modestly high plateau has experienced folding that is easily seen in the landscape and hides seams of coal deposits below the surface.

Julian and Kamnik Alps in the Northwest

Colliding tectonic plates have pushed up Slovenia's Alps, including the Julian Alps, the Kamnik Alps, the Savinjske

Alps and the Karavanke. The country's northwest corner shares features of other European Alps – cliff-hugging trails, crisp breezes, and crystal-clear streams amid high grassy pasturelands. Much of this region sits more than 5,000 feet above sea level, above the elevation that trees can grow. In the Julian Alps you can see most of Slovenia's 88 waterfalls that have resulted from an uplift that began about seven million years ago. Eastward squeezing still occurs along Slovenia's most striking and probably most active fault, the Sava Fault.

Dinaric Mountains in the Southwest

About 35 million years ago the Dinaric Mountains started to form, even before the Alps. Now the Range spans many countries in Central Europe. The westernmost Slovenian part is home to the rare geologic phenomenon Karst, which means landforms that have developed over readily water-soluble rock types. Limestone karst covers almost half of Slovenia, yielding not only 7500 caves, but also disappearing lakes, sink holes and small scale features like rills (little streams or brooks). "Dolina" or valley and "polje" or field have come into the geologic vocabulary through the study of the Slovenian karst region.

Age of rocks

Quaternary period / 0 to 2.5 million years /
Tertiary period / 65 to 2.5 million years /
Mesozoic era / 248 to 65 million years /
Palaeozoic era / 590 to 248 million years /

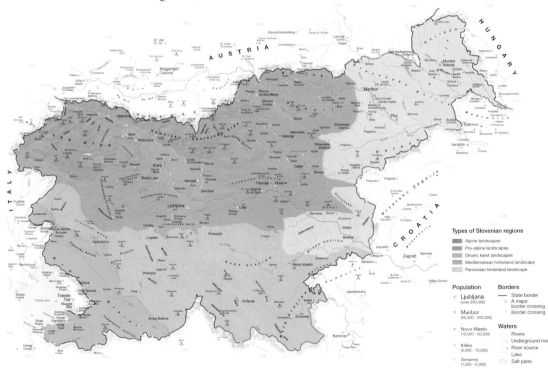

Types of Slovenian regions

Alpine landscapes
Pre-alpine landscapes
Dinaric karst landscapes
Mediterranean hinterland landscape
Pannonian hinterland landscape

Population	Borders
Ljubljana (over 200,000)	State border
Maribor (50,000 - 200,000)	A major border crossing / Border crossing
Novo Mesto (10,000 - 50,000)	Waters
Krško (5,000 - 10,000)	Rivers / Underground rivers / River source / Lake
Šentjernej (1,000 - 5,000)	Salt pans

Just thirty miles south of Ljubljana, Postojna caves boast twelve miles of karst features, open to the public for viewing. Discovery of "the human fish," *proteus anguinus*, in Postojna's nether regions prompted the sudy of cave-dwelling species and the science of speleobiology. About fifteen miles further southwest the United National Educational, Scientific and Cultural Organization, UNESCO, has preserved Skocjan caves as a World Heritage site.

Low rolling hills in the Southeast

Farmlands and thick forests blanket the low-lying Bela Krajina in southeastern Slovenia, situated between the Sava Folds, the Dinaric Mountains, and the Pannonian Basin. The Gorjanci Hills along the Croatian border arose as a set of east-west elevations that were squeezed up along a reactivated Pannonian fault. From there the landscape drops off sharply into the Bela Krajina depression that forms the south-facing Gorjanci-Bela Krajina escarpment.

Otočec castle

Pannonian Basin, Pohorje Hills in the Northeast

The flat landscapes of eastern Slovenia resemble the Hungarian plains because geologically both Hungary and eastern Slovenia belong to the Pannonian Basin. The low-lying ground, consisting of layers of sand, mud, lime and gravel that were deposited in the Pannonian Basin, now lies beneath the rolling hills in the Pannonian region.

The Pohorje Hills in northeast Slovenia contain older, resistant, thermally formed rocks that have been brought to the surface during Pannonian rifting. Much of the medium gray building stone and street curbing around Ljubljana comes from tonalite igneous rock that has been quarried from the core of the Pohorje Hills. Some of the ancient Pannonian faults have reactivated, squeezing up some modest east-west trending hills like the Haloze and Bohor Hills near the Croatian border. Most of the hot springs in Slovenia relate to the high heat flow under the thin, warmed, rifted crust of the Pannonian Basin.

Hills at Ljutomer and Ormož

Telltale Landscapes

These 13 vantage points give you the chance to see tectonics at work in Slovenia. At these spots you cannot only enjoy the scenic beauty, but also detect the natural processes that created it.

All twelve are easily accessible, almost all of them by car, and with refreshments available nearby.

a. Ljubljana Castle Hill

Ljubljana's castle perches on top of a sunken Dinaric mountain peak. From there you can see the low-lying Ljubljana basin surrounding it in all directions.

The best view is north-northwest toward the Alps. The river Sava turns east just north of Ljubljana, having formed a wide bed by leaving thick deposits of sediment it picked up during its course through the mountains.

Walk, bike or drive. An open-air café in the courtyard offers refreshments.

Ljubljana castle

b. Šmarna Gora Peak

About 15 miles northwest of Ljubljana

Ljubljana's most popular "mountain" hut is on top of Šmarna Gora, one of the partially sunken and buried Dinaric mountaintops. An hour's walk lets you to feel as though you have climbed a much higher mountain, since the mountain has sunk down and its base has been covered by sediment.

You will walk along a well-worn trail through a beech and fir forest. The start of a Šmarna Gora trail is located in the village of Tacen and can easily be reached by a Ljubljana city bus.

c. Kamnik Knoll

About 15 miles northwest of Ljubljana in the Kamnik-Savinjski Alps of north Slovenia

From the ruins of Kamnik castle, you can see the meeting of Alps and plains as well as one of the major fault lines in Slovenia. On a clear day you can see across the Ljubljana basin and its marshes to the south, and all the way into the karst regions to the southwest.

Refreshments can be obtained at a nearby gostilna. Drive, bike or walk, but the short road is narrow and winding.

Kamnik

Lake Bohinj

d. Vogel Mountain

About 50 miles northwest of Ljubljana

At the top of Vogel mountain you are in the mostly bare, high Julian Alps, where an active uplift in the rock structure is occurring. Notice that the rocks here are no longer horizontal, but are highly tilted and folded. From above you can see Lake Bohinj, the largest permanent lake in Slovenia. The Bohinj Valley was formed by glacial erosive processes. The terminal depression made by the Bohinj glacier filled with water to make the lake.

Food and lodging are available at the summit in all seasons. Take the gondola, or walk. Ski in winter.

e. Bohinj Valley Floor

About 50 miles northwest of Ljubljana

Giant boulders rolled around by glaciers during the Ice Age and now lie scattered about the region. You can see them and piles of glacial rubble known as moraine on easy walks near Ukanc at the western tip of Lake Bohinj.

No glaciers exist here today, and even the small glaciers in the high Julian Alps are melting due to global warming.

Walk, bike or cross-country ski.

f. Škocjan Caves

About 50 miles southwest of Ljubljana.

Witness hidden underground landscapes in the UNESCO World Heritage Skocjan caves. The river Reka has sculpted passages, chambers and canyons adorned with stalactites and stalagmites.

Please see "Southwest, West, Coast and Karst" section for more information.

You can get refreshments or full meals at the local gostilna near the park entrance. Walk, bike or drive around the park and kras region.

g. Socerb Escarpment

About 65 miles from Ljubljana

Here you can see the western edge of the high Kras plateau and the eastern edge of the low-lying Dinaric flysch basin. This boundary is geologically inactive, but it is a topographically impressive contact because of the differing weathering properties of the neighboring rocks. The walkway along the wall around Socerb castle perches on the ridge's edge and gives you sweeping views of the Bay of Trieste.

Reserve in advance for a sit-down meal at the restaurant, or just have a cool drink at the bar.

Walk, bike or drive.

Socerb Escarpment

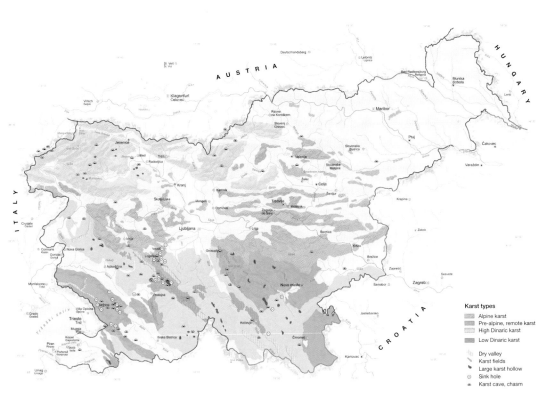

h. Flysch Cliffs at Strunjan

Walking from Strunjan to Piran along the Adriatic coast will provide you with a good view of the flysch rock formations on the cliffs that rise up around the Piran Peninsula. Alternating layers of sandstone and mudstone have been deposited, tilted, bent and faulted during the Dinaric mountain building event. Looking south from the town of Piran you can also see flysch cliffs.

Walk or bike.

Strunjan Cliff

i. Celje Castle Hill

About 50 miles northeast of Ljubljana

The castle at Pečovnik gives a good view of the Sava Folds region with its high topography and east-west wrinkles due to active north-south shortening. These are alpine foothills - the transition between Alps and Dinaric mountains - as well as being the Adria-Eurasia plate boundary.

The castle is under restoration, is accessible by horseback and has a café.

j. Mount Kum

About 50 miles east of Ljubljana

From this highest peak in the Sava Folds region you can see waves of folded hills that mark the alpine hill or transitional region of the Alps and Dinaric Mountains. Like the view from Celje, high topography and east-west wrinkles are due to north-south shortening.

Look to the north for a splendid stretch of the Alps if the winds are right.

A restaurant awaits your arrival at the top, and your radio reception will be great. Bike or walk.

k. Gorjanci Escarpment

About 60 miles southeast of Ljubljana

In these hills you can detect recent uplift. Beech forests blanket the 60-mile long mountain range, and two primeval forest reserves are protected on the northern slopes.

European footpath E7 crosses through this area.

Gorjanci

Ptuj by night

l. Ptuj Castle

About 80 miles northeast of Ljubljana

From the top of the knoll of Ptuj's castle you can see across the river Drava valley and into the Haloze Hills. The Pannonian Plains stretch to and beyond the Hungarian border. The earth's crust has been stretched thin here, in a phenomenon reverse to the continental collision that produced the Alps. Notice the low ground all around you.

Walk or bike.

m. The Drava River Road

About 80 miles northeast of Ljubljana to Maribor

Through hilly topography and the river gorge, the advantage to the road from Maribor to Dravograd is that it tightly follows the river Drava for the entire run of about 40 miles. You can see over a prolonged time and space how the River has carved and sculpted the valley. The Italian Drave begins its 450 mile journey in the south Tyrol, flows across Austria's Carinthia, through Slovenia and into Croatia and Hungary, joining the Danube at Osijek.

Drive or bike.

Abundant Parklands

M uch of the terrain that you can view from the 13 vantage points above can also be accessed by foot, ski
or bicycle trails. More than 80 nature and tourist trails run
about 250 miles within the country. This section will acquaint you with a few parks and paths. Please check the web
for updates just before your trip.

For active travel, parklands can offer you recreation in
scenery rich with scientific intrigue. Those that are harder
to reach may hold particular allure for pioneering types who

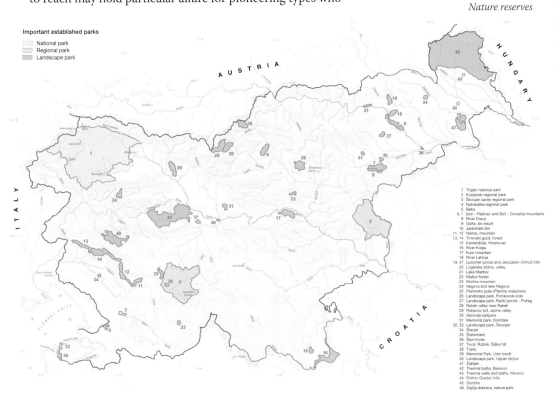

Nature reserves

Important established parks
- National park
- Regional park
- Landscape park

1 Triglav national park
2 Kozjanski regional park
3 Škocjan caves regional park
4 Notranjska regional park
5 Beka
6, 7 Boč - Plešivec and Boč - Donačka mountains
8 River Drava
9 Golte, ski resort
10 Jareninski dol
11, 12 Nanos, mountain
13, 14 Trnovski gozd, forest
15 Kamenščak, Hrastovec
16 River Kolpa
17 Kum mountain
18 River Lahinja
19, 47 Ljutomer ponds and Jeruzalem-Ormož hills
20 Logarska dolina, valley
21 Lake Maribor
22 Mašun forest
23 Mrzlica mountain
24 Negova and lake Negova
25 Planinsko polje (Planina meadows)
26 Landscape park, Ponikovski kras
27 Landscape park, Rački ponds - Požeg
28 Rakek valley near Rakek
29 Robanov kot, alpine valley
30 Sečovlje saltpans
31 Memorial park, Domžale
32, 33 Landscape park, Strunjan
34 Štanjel
35 Štatenberk
36 Šturmovec
37 Tivoli, Rožnik, Šiška hill
38 Topla
39 Memorial Park, Udin boršt
40 Landscape park, Upper Idrijca
41 Zabljek
42 Thermal baths, Banovci
43 Thermal wells and baths, Moravci
44 Polhov Gradec hills
45 Goričko
46 Zajčja dobrava, nature park

prefer remote serenity. Slovenia has undertaken a vigorous program to preserve its wealth of natural resources. One national, two regional, 38 landscape and 26 Natura 2000 Areas have been already set aside for preservation. With international help from entities like UNESCO and the European Union, many more are in the planning stages. Slovenian lands offer great opportunities to bike, canoe, swim, hike, ski, and study in unspoiled settings.

The Natura 2000 parks conform to European Union legislation that is designed to protect the most seriously threatened habitats and species across Europe. One directive helps protect and manage areas for the breeding, feeding, wintering or migration of rare and vulnerable birds. The other protects and manages rare and vulnerable animals, plants and habitats.

Landscape Parks fall under the **Protected Forest Areas** rules. As defined by the European Landscape Convention, "landscape" means an area whose character derives from the interaction between natural and human factors. In Europe one of the primary purposes of forest protection is to protect characteristic landscapes.

Mountains and rivers tend to be chosen for protection. Since rivers sometimes mark borders, parks often follow the country's boundary lines. Trail maps are provided on site in brochures and large-scale posters.

Ljubljana Area. Around Ljubljana you can easily reach a surprising number of places with natural interest. Šmarna Gora to the northwest offers an easy "alpine" experience.

South of Ljubljana lie the lowland marshes, a favorite biking area. Not far from the old Roman settlements of Ig and Iska Vas, European Footpaths E6 and E7 intersect at the village of Rakitna, known for its crystal clear lake and air.

Northwest. Triglav National Park in the Julian Alps tops the list in size and history, having been conceived as early as 1908. It is the park that offers a glass of beer or a piece of strudelj as you make your way across rugged high country. Its natural beauty has long been guarded, while paths and lodges have been built to better enjoy it.

Other less known mountains to the north that offer the same kinds of amenities include the Karavanke that borders Austria, and the Kamnisko-Savinjske Alps just below the Karavanke. Logarska Dolina Landscape Park offers opportunities for hiking, biking, horseback-riding and mountain climbing, as well as wintertime activities in an extensive, alpine setting. Velika Planina an alpine plateau speckled with dairy farm huts, draws skiers and hikers all the year-round.

Southwest. To the southwest lie the fascinating kras or karst phenomena, with rivers that disappear into the rocks to reappear at the sea after carving underground caves and channels. Curiosities here have intrigued emperors and adventurers alike. Biking and hiking in these lands allows closer examination of sunken valleys, sinkholes, and the myriad other characteristics associated with the kras.

Škocjan Regional Park, a UNESCO Heritage Site, is well worth planning into your visit.

Northeast. The river Mura banks along the Croatian border, the Pohorja Mountains west of Maribor, the Haloze Hills below Ptuj all are sites in the planning for official parkland designations..

Kozjanski Landscape Park has recently been developed as a park, now about half of the area designated for eventual preservation. You can take a walk and see 21 points of geologic significance using a guidebook prepared by UNESCO and the Ministry for the Environment.

Southeast. European long distance footpaths cross the Gorjanci Ridges and canoes ply the Kolpa River with local guides Kočevski Rog – the Horn of Kočevje - considered the wildest territory of Slovenia, has long been inaccessible to tourists due to previous military activities. Animal life in the Kočevje hills thus counts among the least disturbed. Check for updates on accessibility to this area.

Triglav flower (Potentilla nitida)

European Footpaths E6 and E7

Two trans-continental footpaths cross the entire country, intersecting south of Ljubljana near the town of Rakitna. European Footpath E6 links the Baltic to the Adriatic, beginning in Finland, traversing Sweden, Denmark, Germany, Austria, Slovenia and ending in Greece. E6 comes into Slovenia's north at Radlje ob Dravi and runs to the Adriatic Sea. Allow 14 days walking time.

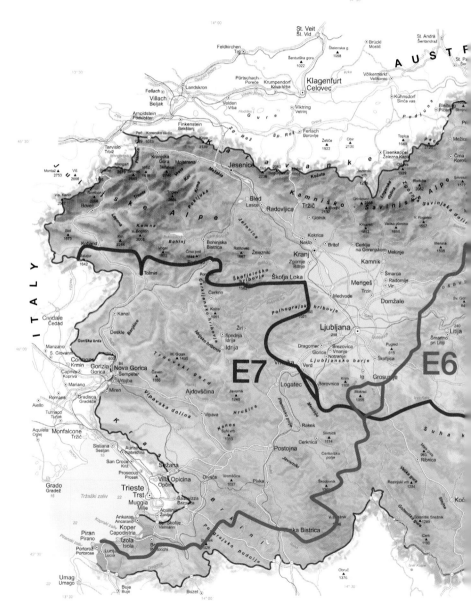

E7 starts in Spain and crosses Andorra, France, Italy, Slovenia, and exits into Hungary. From Kobarid at the Italian border, D7 runs to the Hungarian border at Hodoš and takes about 21 days to walk. Together E6 and E7 total about 600 miles in Slovenia, mainly through forested areas, and intersect some 25 miles south of Ljubljana.

Toplice – Hot Springs Health Resorts

Luxury in natural settings.

The tectonic plates that push up the Alps in the west create a hotplate effect in the east by stretching and thinning the earth's crust into plains. Naturally heated mineral waters flow just below the surface and spring forth here and there. From Roman times onward, inhabitants of the area that is now Slovenia have recognized and enjoyed the benefits of these subterranean streams.

You can probably find 20 or more thermal resorts in the country. The five showcased in this section offer complete services. You can stay at any one of them for a whole week and have friends and family visit you there. Massage, sauna, dining rooms, cafés, parks, bike paths and hiking trails are but a few of the amenities that will allow you to set yourself up for a prolonged wellness experience.

Air and water jets spray cyclically for full-body or back and neck massage. You can exercise by swimming against the current or sweeping along with it. Try a variety of temperatures by switching from pool to pool. Before heading back to your apartment, bungalow or room, you might just crawl onto a lounge chair and snooze.

Slovenians consider thermal spas as a necessary part of healthcare, both for vigorous physical workouts and relaxed rejuvenation. Heavy emphasis is placed on physical fitness throughout life, especially swimming. You will share the facilities with people of all ages.

Often more traditional therapeutic services are available as well. Clinics on site offer medical staff to gear therapies to individual needs. Foods available in the complexes tend to be organic and wellness-oriented.

< Rogaška Slatina

Slovenia's spas throughout the country offer a luxurious, healthful way to enjoy the country's natural treasures. You can find some spas in the west too. Bled in the northwest and Portorož and Strunjan in the southwest, for example, offer thermal bath spas.

Snovik, just a half hour's drive from Ljubljana, brings a brand new facility to ancient hot springs that the locals have enjoyed for decades. A glass-covered dome encloses thermal pools for year-round swimming by day and night. On-site lodging and a restaurant add to the convenience of physiotherapy, saunas and massage services available within the complex. The picturesque town of Kamnik lies a few miles to the west for shopping and dining excursions.

Terms usually include unlimited acess to all pools, with extras like massage and various therapies at additional cost. Look for notices of bike rentals, regional tours, health and exercise classes and special events close to the reception area.

Thermal baths, Snovik

At **Dobrna**'s new hotel you can swim under the stars. The whole pool complex can be accessed from the hotel without ever going outside. As you might imagine, this resort becomes especially popular in cold weather, when pheasant and venison goulash are served at nearby gostilnas. Saturday night's live music here draws serious dancers from Celje, Maribor and beyond.

Dobrna

In the **Moravske Toplice** resort (also known as Terme 3000) you have the choice of apartment, bungalow, hotel room or suite. You can reach one of Slovenia's best wine roads within half an hour. Rent a bike at the resort and ride on trails well off the road to charming villages where the storks nest.

Moravske Toplice

Massage therapy comes by air and water jets that cycle through different areas. Here bathers have gathered to the semi-circle of all over massage bubblers. Inside pools of varying temperatures afford shade and shelter. Outside pools offer sun-drenched attractions like slides and water currents. Water aerobics classes bring together those with common interests and abilities.

The castle museum in nearby Murska Sobota, also home to the specialty dessert gibanica, merits a visit. Close to the Hungarian and Croatian borders, language, food and custom, the resort complex is styled in the Hungarian thatch-roof fashion.

Šmarješke Toplice tucks into deep lush woods. Large outdoor wooden tubs are set in park-like surroundings of old-growth forests. The spa complex offers a variety of accommodations, including hotel, bungalows, and apartments.

Nearby Otočec castle hotel in the middle of the river Krka is linked by common ownership. You can easily combine the two or split your time between them. The resort offers many excursions to neighboring sights as well.

Dolenjske Toplice offers a big new indoor-outdoor pool connected to the resort hotels by a promenade through a lime tree and chestnut allée. The renovated Austrian era buildings have their own thermal baths in the lower levels. In the dining room you will find herbal teas and juices along with fruits and grains. A garden café occupies the center of the cluster, and a popular restaurant is hidden along the wooded walk.

Šmarješke Toplice

Krško hills

Thermal Talk

Veliki bazen – *large pool*
Mali bazen – *small pool*
Temperatura – *temperature*
Voda – *water 30–31 degrees Centigrade*
Zrak – *air*
Temperature – *temperature*
Voda – *water 31 degrees Centigrade*
Samo bosi – *bare feet only*

Priporočamo večkratno 15 minutno kopanje v bazenu – *We recommend 15 minutes bathing in the pools at a time (SLO, Italian, German) – Si consiglia il bagno in acquatermale per 15 minuti pui volte, con intervalli – Es wird empolen sich im termalwassert jedesmal nicht langer als 15 minuten aufzuhalten*

Za neplavalce – *literally "for non-swimmers," meaning no swimming in this particular pool*
Za plavalce – *for swimmers*
Reševalec iz vode – *"Rescuer from the water" or lifeguard*
Obvezno tuširanje – *compulsory shower*
V tem prostoru ne kadimo! – *don't smoke in this area*
WC or "stranišče" – *the little place off to the side*

Prinašanje in uživanje hrane in pijač v prostorih kopališča ni dovoljeno! – *It is prohibited to bring or consume food and drink into this bathhouse area.*

Vhod garderobe – *entrance*
Izhod – *exit*
Sušenje las – *hair dryer*
Tobogan – *water slide*
Skupinske garderobe – *dressing areas for groups*
Pozor! Spolzka tla – *be careful! slippery floor*
vodna masaža – *water massage*
aerobika – *aerobics*
fizioterapija – *physiotherapy*
bazen za otroke – *children's pool*
tuš – *shower*
vhod – *entrance*
izhod – *exit*
skakanje prepovedano – *diving prohibited*
tobogan – *water slide*
blagajna – *cashier*
vstopnica – *ticket*

Finding SLOVENIA
The Essence of Slovenia

reševalec – *life guard*
kopalke – *swimming suit*
cenik – *price list*
kopalni plašč – *swimming robe*

Terme Čatež

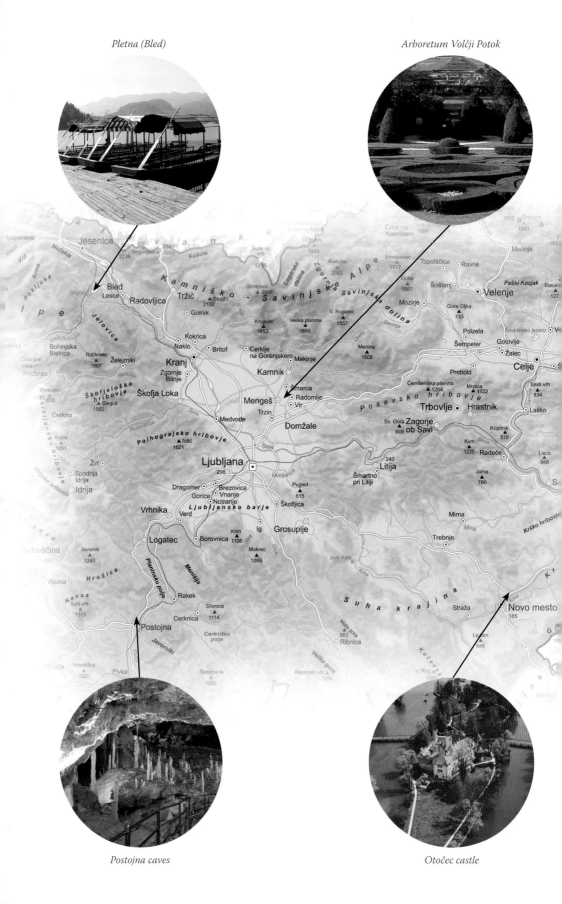

Pletna (Bled)

Arboretum Volčji Potok

Postojna caves

Otočec castle

A Heart and Four Corners

Ljubljana – A Jewel Beyond All

*N*ow that you have a sense of Slovenia as a whole, you might enjoy seeing some regional distinctions. The following section will look first at Ljubljana and then each of four corners, counterclockwise starting with the northwest. In this way you may see what vast variety exists in such a small space and also gather more information to tailor your travel to suit your interests.

The format for Ljubljana and the four corners of Slovenia resembles a mosaic. Small pieces are arranged to give an overall impression. A collage of highlights is intended to convey complexities brought about by a long and diverse history. Please remember that none of the writing pretends to be either comprehensive or objective.

Ljubljana feels like a European city, with old world grace and style. There you will hear the symphony and see stately museums. In the country you will feel the influence of folklore, neighboring and historic influences, and taste local flavors of food, beverage and celebrations. Each area has its own charm. Combining the parts can add spice to your travel experience.

In broad terms, here's the lie of the land.

- Ljubljana: The heart of the country; physical and cultural center
- Northwest: Alps shared with Austria and Italy; emphasis on hiking and skiing
- Southwest: Adriatic Coast and karst inland; resort towns and natural fascination
- Southeast: Wide rivers and wooded hills; wilderness and authenticity
- Northeast: Rolling hills and Pannonian plains; Eastern influence and thermal spas

< Mid-Slovenia - Between the marsh, mountains and valleys

With unpretentiously classic style, Ljubljana lies at the heart of Slovenia, in location as well as almost every other respect. Activity centers here, intellectually, culturally, culinarily, politically and socially. Not only do all roads lead to the central city, but the quickest way to reach other parts of Slovenia often means going through Ljubljana.

Historically the site on the river below the hill has attracted settlers from all directions. The city seems to be a museum of references to its past. Illyrians were the Stone Age settlers in the Ljubljana marshes, and the Illyrian Provinces were part of Napoleon's 19th century realm. The city's history ties into the Greek myth of Jason and the Golden Fleece. Emona is Ljubljana's former name under the Romans. You may notice allusions to these eras as you walk the streets.

Ljubljana bows to those whose inspiration has led through times of oppression, poverty and hardship. Words, architecture, art and music have been the vehicles of Valvasor, Prešeren, Cankar, Plečnik, Gallus. These are names

Ljubljana

Ljubljana castle, with the Slovenian National Theatre from the mid-19th century below

you will see honored throughout the entire country, but particularly in the capital.

A map will orient you with a few key locations like the castle, Prešeren Square, the public market, Congress Square, the University, museums and Tivoli Park, and show how these locations relate to the river Ljubljanica. The most important subject appears at the end. Education has played a key role in the history of the country and continues to strengthen the fibers that bind it together in nationhood. Ljubljana, as the country's major city, reflects this most notably.

Jason and the Dragon

A couple of years ago when I was in the vicinity of Ljubljana's medieval theater, a familiar emblem caught my eye. It looked as though it could not be there just by accident, having been forged of wrought iron and permanently fixed.

According to classical legend, the Greek Prince Jason stole the Golden Fleece from the King of Thessaly. Then he fled with his companions, the Argonauts.

The connection lies in the escape. His route took him from the Black Sea to the Danube, Sava and Ljubljanica rivers. At about Ljubljana's present location, Jason slew a

Zmajski most (Dragon Bridge)

dragon. That is why you see the dragon gracing Ljubljana's coat of arms, acting as the city's mascot and guarding the bridge near the public market.

France Prešeren, Poet

For the past 150 years, the poet France Prešeren has retained preeminent stature in the minds and hearts of Slovenians. In the early 1800s Prešeren brought home to his native country a newly discovered European intellectualism, gained from his studies of law in Vienna. At a time when Slovenia's literary growth had been stunted by politics, Prešeren's elegant style, sensitivity and lyricism struck a chord that has reverberated all the way into the twenty-first century.

Prešeren's poetry expresses love for his land and a longing that arises from personal losses. Some of his poems wrestle with the dilemma of accepting other cultural

To a World of Peace

Here's to the birth of that bright new day
when every nation will awaken
to see the sun's rays fall
on an earth free of strife,
full of shared kinship, and
devoid of ill-will.

Slovene National Anthem
By France Prešeren (J. Widmar Stewart)

France Prešeren monument

trappings without losing Slovenian identity. The theme of water, a primary feature of the country's landscape, brings rhythms of storms and waves to his writing.

Hidden messages add allegorical meaning to his sonnets. In one poem he encrypted the name of his unrequited love Julija Primic by beginning each verse with one letter of her name. The most famous of his writings is sung by all Slovenians as the hallmark of their identity.

A national cultural holiday commemorates France Prešeren each February 8th. On that day his verses are read in front of his statue in Ljubljana, in public places and private homes. You will see tribute paid to him throughout the country, even in the furthest outlying villages.

Ivan Cankar – Author, Playwright, Poet

Ivan Cankar (1876 – 1918) wrote such poignant satire of oppression and social injustice that he was imprisoned by the Austrian Imperial government. A champion for those who were cast out, he chose topics that dramatized their plight in his many dramas, short stories, articles, novels and verse. In a style sometimes likened to James Joyce and Franz Kafka, he employed symbolism in his works with political and cultural themes.

Born a tailor's son, he studied architecture in Vienna, and continued living there to begin his writing career. As a freelance writer, he was soon able to support himself with his writings. In 1907 he returned to Slovenia.

Ivan Cankar

To appreciate Cankar's best-known work *Yerney's Justice*, or *The Bailiff Yerney*, written in 1907 and translated in 1926, it is invaluable to understand the times and the literal translation of the title, *Hlapec Jernej*. "Hlapec" means "bailiff" in the English sense of the word: an overseer of an estate, a steward. The word derives from the Latin bajulus, meaning "person in charge."

Until the end of World War I the feudal system had held sway in Central Europe.

Picture a storybook setting.

A chestnut tree-lined trail leads to the medieval castle high on a wooded hill.
Columned porticos herald the market halls with a flutter of flowers and red umbrellas.
In the shadows of three bridges terraced bistros stow away.
Cobblestone ways wind to inns and merchants, giving glimpses of hidden garden walls.
Along the riverwalk booksellers purvey their fares by the balustrades
As sentinel lindens shade by day, share by dark.
Meet a colleague. Find a friend.
Ask and answer the endless quest, "What's the latest?"
Ever the currency most common, words flow as freely as the waters below,
echoing into times long gone and those to come.
(If you have trouble pronouncing "Ljubljana," as many do, just say "A Jewel Beyond All.")

The Austrian Empire ran on the steam of its vassals. If a lord had a good reliable manager to run his castle or manor house, he could be gone for years at a time and come home to a perfectly managed property

In Cankar's novel, Jernej served as the bailiff of a noble's estate throughout his entire life. Now he is old. His master dies, leaving the domain to his son who tells Jernej he's no longer of use and must leave. After spending his whole life faithfully improving and managing the property for his former master, old Jernej finds himself an outcast. He sets out to find justice, believing that there must be some law to reward him in his old age with a roof over his head and food in his mouth after a lifetime of committed service. His quest is met with derision and scorn. At the end, he sets the building on fire, and is thrown into it by those adhering to the old system of aristocratic justice.

Here is a brief excerpt from "Bailiff Jernej, *The Bailiff Yerney*.

The Bailiff Yerney
Ivan Cankar

"Pity! I do not knock at the door of pity, but at that of justice, in order that it shall open for me – very wide, too. He who has managed a farm during forty years is neither a beggar nor a vagabond; he who has built a house himself is not homeless; he who has cultivated extensive fields need not beg for bread. If you have worked, your toil is yours; that is the law. I'll find justice; justice must be done by me.

(Translated from the Slovene by Sidonie Years, H.C.Sewell Grant, Državna Založba Slovenije, Ljubljana 1968.)

Jože Plečnik, Master Architect

It is by no casual chance that the classic elegance of **Jože Plečnik**'s white-pillared pavilions and balustraded bridges became the essence of Ljubljana. By careful calculation Plečnik created a national look that would endow Slovenia with its own cultural legitimacy.

Drawing from the history of the land, he chose the grandeur of Roman temples and the quiet simplicity of the Italian Renaissance. He added flourishes from the Baroque and bright, square openness from the Mediterranean. He brought his Viennese studies to the style, as well as his vision of Ljubljana as a new Athens, all the while striving to keep alive the age-old Slovak-Slovenian rustic heritage of ancient Carantania.

Plečnik's work intertwines north, south, east and west. At critical points of intersection, the river and the bridges play a major role. They set the stage for people to gather, mingle and stroll.

Plečnik cloaked Ljubljana's castle hill and river town in soft green. He used parks, squares, tree-lined walkways, and flowers to unify old and new sectors. Tivoli Park, Congress Square, the marketplace, the national library, the Žale cemetery all reflect his public purpose. Through education, he sought to instill in his students too the social role of architecture and the importance of preserving historic landmarks. The school of architecture Plečnik founded in Ljubljana still attests to his influence.

Plečnik's design leadership manifested itself early on. Although he was expected to follow in his father's footsteps as a cabinet-maker, he accepted instead a scholarship for the newly opened industrial arts and crafts school in Graz,

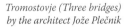

Tromostovje (Three bridges) by the architect Jože Plečnik

Austria. An architect at the school arranged for him to design and produce furniture in Vienna.

While in Vienna, Plečnik attended an exhibition of Otto Wagner's plans for a cathedral in Berlin and signed on as his student. From there he worked in three cities, and in each he left monuments of three different stages of his development as an architect: Vienna, Prague and Ljubljana. In Vienna he designed the Zacherl Palace. As the castle architect in Prague he oversaw the 15-year restoration project of the Hradcani fortress. When at the age of 50 he returned to his native Slovenia as a professor. World War I had just ended. Greatly invigorated by the formation of the new Kingdom of Slovenians, Croats and Serbs that occurred after the break-up of the Austro-Hungarian Empire, he developed a preeminent plan for Slovenia's premier city.

Plečnik died in 1957. Almost 40 years later, in 1996, an exhibition of his work was displayed at the George Pompidou Center in Paris, then taken to Ljubljana, Madrid, Munich, Karlsruhe, Milan, Venice, New York and Washington. A permanent showing is available to the public at

National and University Library in Ljubljana in 1936, by the architect Jože Plečnik

the Museum of Architecture at the Fuzine Castle Museum of Architecture.

Grad Fužine

If you're renting a car after your stay in Ljubljana, think about stopping at Grad Fužine on the way out of town. Situated in a serene spot between a park and the Ljubljanica river, the 16th century castle Grad Fužine, is adorned with towers on each of its four corners and over the entrance, reached by a stone walkway over a moat.

It's a bit tricky to find, so make sure you have a good map and cross the bridge lined with Plečnik's signature lamp posts.

Fužine castle

Inside the Castle Chapel

The walls and ceiling of the chapel tell stories beyond the names they recite. "Isterreich," an old form of "Ostreich" means the eastern empire, and "Windischmarck" refers to the windisch people, as Slovenian ancestoral tribes were called. "Marck" denotes mark or march, the buffer lands or outer edges of the empires. For the Romans they were the lands of first defense against raids from the east. For Austria's eastern empire, castles were fortified mainly as defense stations against the Turkish threat.

Perhaps most striking in the lists of names and standards is the mention of only one bishop, Christoph Rauber of Ljubljana, or Laibach, as it was known in 1530. All the rest are nobles.

Johann Anton Furst zu Eggenberg, 1637, held sway at one of the most important castles. The first Roman settlement in the area, Poetovio, was known as Pettau in the 1600s and now as Ptuj. Prince Eggenberg lived there after the Salzburg archbishops and before the 17th century Hungarian/Scot Walter Leslie.

"Maria Theresia, Queen of Hungary and Bohemia, Archduchess of the East, who came to rule in 1740," stands out as the only woman named in the murals. The lands were divided into duchies, under the control of various dukes who presided from their castles.

Also honored on the murals is Ulrich Graf von Cilly 1565, one of the Counts of Celje who rose to nobility in the 1400s, "Cilly" being the German for Celje.

Look back to Prešeren Square from the river's lower terrace, take the train, funicular or footpath, up to the castle hill.

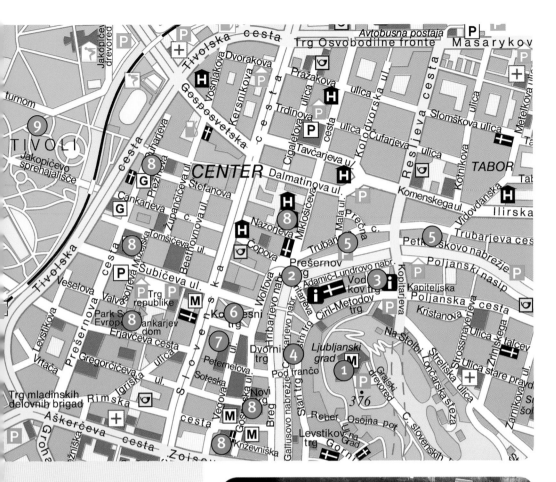

A Walk Around Ljubljana

1. The Castle
2. Three Bridges, Prešeren Square
3. The Market
4. Old Town
5. Riverwalks
6. Congress Square
7. The University
8. Museums and Performance Halls
9. Park Tivoli

Tivoli Park with its palace, Ljubljana

Secessionist Style

When you are standing in Prešeren Square near Tromo-stovje (Three Bridges) in the heart of Ljubljana, look up away from the market to see the Hauptmann House. Built in 1873, the building was the only one in the square to make it through the 1895 earthquake that leveled a good part of the city. Architect Ciril Metod Koch (named after the Macedonian brothers who brought the written word to the Slavic peoples) designed the exterior in the Viennese Secessionist style.

At the turn of the 20th century, the Secessionist style, as it is known in Slovenia, pulled together art forms in an attempt to achieve the harmony of the whole. Also known as art nouveau, Jugendstil and Modernism, the style reflected new ideals and lighter expression. The name represents a breaking away from designs long dominated by classical Greek and Roman influences.

In Ljubljana, the 1901 Dragon Bridge (Zmajski most, with "most" meaning bridge) led the way into the new style. You can see the bridge at the far end of the market. Buildings along Miklošič Street followed the trend. Take a walk up toward Hotel Union from Prešeren Square and continue along that street to view several examples. The bright red one on your right will let you know you're going in the right direction.

Zmajski most (Dragon Bridge), Ljubljana

Old Market, Ljubljana

Old Town

If the door is ajar, walk into City Hall in the Old Town Square to see the beauty of the galleried interiors and a display of Ljubljana's urban plans.

Cafés, shops and buildings follow the small pedestrian street from City Square deeper into Old Town.

Most buildings had to be rebuilt after the 1511 earthquake, but an earlier charm still infuses life along the narrow cobbled paths.

This baroque fountain symbolizing the Sava, Ljubljanica and Krka rivers, stands near City Hall. The Venetian-born sculptor Francesco **Robba** (1698-1757), spent his life primarily in Ljubljana.

Robba fountain in the Town square, Ljubljana

Congress Square

Kongresni trg, 'Congress Square' holds a legacy from the time when Slovenia was part of Napoleon Bonaparte's Illyrian Provinces from 1809 to 1813. Ljubljana served as the capital city of the Provinces and Slovenian became one of the official languages. The University opened on Kongresni trg, the first school of higher education in Slovenia.

The name of the square, however, derives from the meeting that took place in Ljubljana after it fell back under Austrian rule. In 1821, the Emperor and Chancellor of Austria, the Czar of Russia and the king of Naples all gathered in Ljubljana to set a course for the future. In honor of the meeting of the Holy Alliance, as it was called, the park was called Congress Square. The Austrian Chancellor Metternich opposed liberal ideas and nationalistic ideals.

The University

It was from the balcony of the main University building facing Congress Square that Slovenia proclaimed independence in 1991. Founded in 1919, the University draws an international student body.

Museums and Concert Halls

One of Ljubljana's greatest musical legacies marked its 300 year anniversary in 2001. The Philharmonicum celebrated by renovating its nineteenth-century building on Congress Square and installing the pipe organ that was envisaged by architect Jose Plečnik in 1936.

Still considered as one of Europe's foremost orchestras, the Philharmonic claims a distinguished history. Since its founding in 1701, it names Ludwig van Beethoven, Niccolò Paganini and Johannes Brahms as honorary members.

University Palace

Beethoven's score for the Pastoral Symphony and his letter of thanks for the honorary membership, form part of the collection of Ljubljana's National University Library. The first honorary member Joseph Haydn presented the philharmonic society with a score of his composition, Missa in Tempore belli (Kriegsmesse; Paukenmesse), in C Major, in

National Museum of Slovenia, was built during the period 1883-1885, Ljubljana

1796. Gustav Mahler served as conductor and pianist in the 1881-82 season. The Czech violist and conductor Václav Talich (1883-1961) led the orchestra after the formation of the Slovenian Philharmonic in 1908.

Included among the more recent tours, the orchestra has visited , Vienna, Rome, Florence, Venice, Zurich, Bern, Geneva, Brussels, Copenhagen, Madrid, Budapest, Prague, Warsaw, Bucharest, St. Petersburg, Moscow, as well as cities in the United States.

On the following pages you will see an example of the art on display in the National Gallery in Ljubljana. Other museums within walking distance include the Museum of Modern Art, the Theater and Film Museum and the Municipal Museum.

Graduation

If you happen to be in any of Slovenia's cities on the day after the high school students have passed their 'Matura,' you will see the main street shut down and students dancing in the streets. At exactly the same time all over Slovenia the country turns out to celebrate. The Matura is the equivalent of about an American high school education plus two years of college.

School finals celebration dance on the streets of Ljubljana

Early in the morning if you are walking the streets of the city you will not mistake the students for anyone else. They all sport the same shirts and most often make their way along in groups, singing at full voice. Once gathered in the main street at noon, they break into old traditional dancing. Now that Slovenia belongs to the European Union, they also perform Greek, French and other members' dances as well. After the festivities you can easily spot the parents of graduating students by the umbrellas they carry for their students who used them as part of the dances.

Ivan Grohar

Ivan Grohar (1867–1911) distinguished himself as a painter of Slovenian peasant life, bringing a lyrical quality to the medium of landscapes and portraiture. Originally a member of the Škofja Loka group of artists, he developed a style very much his own after the group disbanded.

Ivan Grohar

Ivana Kobilca

Ivana Kobilca (1861–1926) gained a European reputation for her realistic painting. Born into a modest provincial family, she studied in Vienna, Sarajevo, Berlin and Paris, and in Munich with Alois Erdtelt. The Société Nationale des Beaux-Arts in Paris counted her among its members. For a number of years she lived in Sarajevo and painted in the folk art style. Although she may be best known for her realistic style, her later painting tended toward impressionism.

With the American impressionistic artist Mary Cassatt (1844-1926), Ivana Kobilca shares the ability to portray strong bonds between her subjects, presented in an unsentimental yet unmistakable way. Both impart quiet warmth to their scenes, especially those of mothers and children. They choose everyday activities of the times, as in the painting here of the gathering and stringing of spring flower garlands. Others by Kobilca show zither playing, coffee drinking and ironing.

Ivana Kobilca, Summer

Places not to Miss

Technical Museum of Slovenia

Just south of Ljubljana on the edge of its marshlands you will find Bistra castle, now devoted to displaying historic tools and machinery. The buildings bridge a stream where a waterwheel used to operate, but now sits picturesquely on the side.

Cankar Museum and Ballooning in Vrhnika.

An exit off the main toll road southwest of Ljubljana takes you right into Ivan Cankar's hometown of Vrhnika and a museum in his honor. Vrhnika is also the starting point for hot air balloon trips.

Arboretum, Volčji Potok

Arboretum

Twelve miles or so north of Ljubljana, Volčji potok Arboretum lies between Domžale and Kamnik. Established by the University of Ljubljana in 1952, it is now run by the Ministry of Culture. With walkways, motorized train, a garden center, landscape architects and projects all over Slovenia, it claims over 2500 types of trees and an extensive landscape park.

Shopping

Many boutiques and department stores are located downtown and in old town Ljubljana. The giant shopping complex City Park lies northeast of the city.

See also:

Šmarna Gora Peak to the west and the ancient Roman sites of Ig and Iška vas to the south.

Šmarna gora

The Northwest

Slovenia's northwest corner claims an array of natural gems - wooded mountains, high pastures, river valleys, alpine lakes.

Lake Bled. Known for its therapeutic waters, air and light, the international resort town of Lake Bled has drawn visitors to its shores for curative as well as tourist reasons. A top travel-destination, it is second only to Ljubljana in popularity. A variety of pensions, apartments, hotels and restaurants continue the longstanding tradition of welcoming guests. The picture-perfect town nestled on the lakeshore against the backdrop of soaring Alps serves as the gateway to the Julian Alps.

Triglav National Park in the Julian Alps. The idea of preserving the Julian Alps began in 1908, and has been advanced by scientists since that time. Julian alpine traditions stem in large part from botanists who combed the Alps accompanied by mountain guides. An industrialist brother of one early botanist built shelters for their use, thus beginning the long-established custom of mountain huts.

Park rangers of today carry on the heritage of guiding explorers through the far reaches of their lands. From addressing large groups to leading individual hikes, they perform a wide range of functions. Inside the Park you will find marked hiking and ski trails, food, lodging, museums, exhibits, informational placards and posted maps. In Trenta, the heart of the Park, you can find rooms, apartments, camping and gostilnas. From there you can follow the river Soča or hike up the slopes.

Kamnik, Logarska Dolina, Krvavec and Velika Planina share the grandeur of the Kamnisko-Savinjske Alps. Lying

Lake Bled

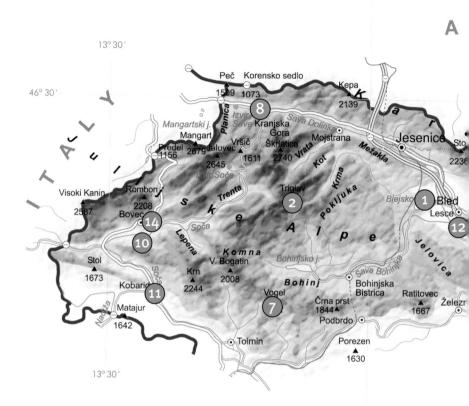

to the north of Ljubljana, all four areas offer magnificent hiking and skiing opportunities.

Quaint towns. A number of towns between Ljubljana and Bled portray rich historical beauty and significance. Museums in Škofja Loka, Kranj and Radovljica merit a visit.

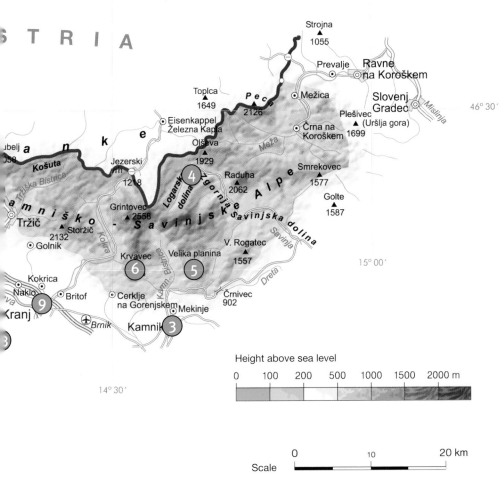

14° 30′

15° 00′

STRIA

Strojna
▲
1055

Prevalje ⊙ Ravne
⊚na Koroškem

Toplca
1649
P e c ▲ ⊙ Mežica
2126
Slovenj
Gradec

Plešivec
⊙ Eisenkappel
Železna Kapla
Olševa
Črna na
Koroškem 1699 ▲ (Uršlja gora)

46° 30′

Mislinja

ubelj a n k e
058
Košuta
Jezerski
vrh
Meža

Raduha
▲
2062
Smrekovec
▲
1577

Grintovec
▲ 2558
Golte
▲
1587

Tržič Storžič
2132
⊙ Golnik

Krvavec
Velika planina
V. Rogatec
▲
1557

Savinja

Dreta

15° 00′

Kokrica
Naklo
9 ⊙ Britof
Cerklje
na Gorenjskem Mekinje
Črnivec
902

Kranj
⊕ Brnik Kamnik 3

4

Logarska dolina
Zgornja Savinjska dolina
Kamniško - Savinjske Alpe
Savinjska dolina

6 **5**

Height above sea level

0   100   200   500   1000 1500 2000 m

0   10   20 km
Scale

Between Venice and Vienna. The award-winning museum at Kobarid is devoted to World War I history, focusing on the 43 years when the political control over the town changed nine times. The border between Italy and Yugoslavia was redrawn in the 1950s to give Trieste to Italy due to the Western fears that the Yugoslavian leader Marshall Tito would allow Russia access to the Adriatic Sea.

Meditation (Duma)
A Fragment

Their backs and shoulders strong as cliffs;
Their necks (a load, O tyrant, you can place thereon)
Will carry all and will not bend.
Their hearts love peace, but they are stout;
Their pride is without words;
As if they are not born of mothers
But from mountains crags had issued forth.
Into the world they go, and foreign lands may boast
Of their hands' work and of their skill.
There – in America, there – in Westphalia
They're lost to us, beyond the reach of sight.
Where are you, native land? Here in the fields
Beneath Triglav? Among the Karavanks?
Among the furnaces and in the mines
Beyond the seas – you who knows no bounds?
There was a time I wished you'd broaden forth,
Expand and spread across the world,
But now it's plain that boundless you have grown;
Like seeds you scatter into distance all your breed.
Will you, like swallows, tempt them home again?
Will they, like doves, unite beneath the roof?
Or will they, once beguiled by might and glory
Of foreign lands, no more return to you?
Where are you, native land? Here in the fields
Beneath Triglav? Among the Karavanks?
Among the furnaces and in the mines
Beyond the seas – you who knows no bounds?
I understand and feel for you. The poet's dream
For many a year has hovered over you,
Watching, listening, weeping, hoping
Your secret to disclose.
The oyster, deep within the sea, its pain intense
Into a gem has gathered.
O poets heart what gathers now in you?
O poet's heart – it is your pain.

Oton Župančič

The Lake

The daily hours that glide across the sky
are mirrored on the waters passing by;
all dawns dip into thee their golden rays,
all stars upon the surface write their ways.
Like many truths they're pictured each and all;
the peak and hill, the steeple, island small,
the bird and cloud, those wanderers to heaven –
out of thy depths all things are doubly given.
The lake thus mirrors glories infinite,
displaying light and shade; a wondrous sight
before our eyes! As idly we look on,
into our inner self these charms are gone.

Oton Župančič

Bled

The Triglav National Park

As you can see from the map, few roads intrude on the tranquility of the National Park and cars share the ones that do with bicyclists and hikers.

Take the gondola at Vogel to reach the slopes for downhill skiing, but you can cross-country ski on the Pokljuka plateau and in the valleys.

Two "Musts" for the Mountains

The Mountain Hut Directory contains a separate page for each of Slovenia's 151 mountain huts. Coded entries for 28 categories gives you quick, precise information such as dates of operation, number of beds, directions and phone number for each hut. An introduction in six languages shows you how to interpret the codes. This exceptionally handy guide covers all of Slovenia, not just the national park, and is produced by the mountaineering society. *Slovenija, Mountain Huts, Berghutten, Rifugi alpini, Planinarski domovi, Horolezecke chatty, Planinska zveza Slovenije*, Ljubljana, 1997.

Triglav dom (home) on Kredarica, the highest mountain hut in Slovenia.

A topographical map showing elevations, caves, natural windows, cliffs, lakes, rivers, waterfalls, glaciers, moors, forests, pastures, hay racks, castles, chair lifts, gondolas, nature reserves, cultural monuments, natural formations, geological routes with observations points, protected plant species, locations of mountain lodging, bus stops, and car parks.

Mountain climbing and hiking in Slovenia are very popular sports.

"Koča" and "Dom" on maps and guides indicate lodging. Either one can have a kitchen or not, so check the mountain hut book for specifics.

Find an extensive selection of maps and guides both at **Kod in Kam** map and bookstore in Ljubljana, close to the University and up from the river. Or look for them at the Triglav National Park Visitor Centers at Bled and Trenta. In downtown Ljubljana, check with Mladinjska Knjiga on the main street, Slovenska Cesta, second floor.

Another excellent book – *Mountaineeering in Slovenia: The Julian Alps, The Kamnik & Savinja Alps, The Kara-vanke* by Tine Mihelič. The book is divided into easy walks, longer trips and challenging high-country trips requiring mountain climbing know-how.

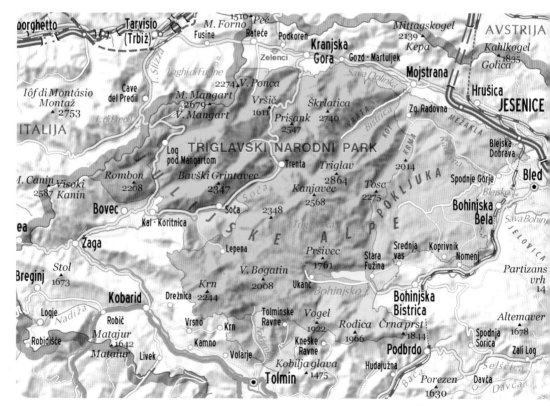

The Triglav National Park

For German speakers, Wolfram Guhl's compact, informative book will show you what scenery to expect in what parts.

Guhl, Wolfram, Nationalpark Triglav, *Ein Bergparadies in Slowenien*, Verlag Carinthia, Klagenfurt, 2004.

Although harder to both find and pack, the 1987 English edition of **The Triglav National Park,** published by Triglavski narodni park gives detailed scientific information on what to find where in the park, including climate, early mountain exploration and its cultural heritage, ethnology of alpine pastoral economy, popular architectural heritage, alpine dairy farming on the Gorenjsko side, cheese-making on sheep pastures and cattle pastures in the Tolmin region.

Prepare for Changing Conditions.

Even on a hot, sunny day, rock trails can be treacherously slick, especially when you face cables and tiny footholds near the end and can't bear to quit without finishing the hike. Wear hiking boots, not just tennis shoes. Carry water. If you are not physically up to the whole undertaking, please forego the glory. Hike only as far your own capacity can carry you.

Lake Lužnica, Julian Alps

Remember, too, the toll of high altitude. Proceed slowly. Stopping at all the watering holes along the way can keep you from all kinds of ills, as well as making the trip far more enjoyable.

Expect heavy traffic to Triglav – literally "Three Heads" - in summer. If you want the park to yourself, go in the spring or fall and start at the Trenta Visitor Center.

Rivers Born of Mountains

Lakes of Glaciers Past

The signature peaks of Triglav immortalized on the national flag, in poetry and song, rise up as the centerpiece of the park. From the mountains spring the rivers that have sculpted the numerous valleys and gorges. Glaciers formed the domed and pyramidal summits, cut windows in rock walls, and left long flat meadows and lakes.

Two of Slovenia's major rivers, the Sava and Soča, both begin in Triglav, and, if you are fit and adventuresome, you can see the source of both. Catch the trail to the Sava source, or "izvir," (pronounced "eez veer" with the accent on the 2nd syllable), about three miles west of the western end of Lake Bohinj. For the Soča source trail, go about five miles up the road from Trenta.

The Soča winds south to the Adriatic Sea, while the Sava heads east to the Black Sea. As a result, the climate along the Soča tends to be Mediterranean, while the Sava brings the harsher Central European alpine and continental conditions. Expect even greater variation between the areas north of Triglav and those to the south. The northern Vrata Valley can be markedly colder than the Trenta Valley. The vegetation and animal life reflects these climatic differences as well.

Bohinj is the largest permanent lake, but there are many subterranean waters that may bear little relation to surface waters. Thus you can see waterfalls that seem to appear from nowhere, and springs that come and go. Triglav has no shortage of full time lakes, however, including the seven Triglav lakes, Kriz Lakes and Krn Lakes.

Julian Alpine Botany

In the tradition of alpine gardens, the Juliana Alpine Botanical Garden was founded in the Trenta Valley in 1926. This long deep wrinkle in the mountains of the southwestern Triglav National Park opens the area to Adriatic influences,

The river Soča valley

The mountains at Bohinj

Daffodils on Golica mountain

thereby tempering the weather and growing conditions. The same plants generally grow 100 feet higher up on the Trenta Valley side than on the harsher Vrata Valley side.

The Alps in northwestern Slovenia have long attracted the attention of scientists. Among the first botanists to explore them was Baron Karel Zois, who discovered both the Zois Bellflower, Campanula zoysii and the Zois' Violet, viola zoysii. In studying and researching the plants, he worked closely with F.X. Wulfen in Klagenfurt, who named the flowers after Zois and wrote about the findings in Viennese anthologies.

As early as 1780, Baron Karel Zois had the first of two mountain huts built in the Julian Alps for studying botany. His brother Žiga, owner of the Bohinj forges and patron of Slovene arts and sciences, financed many of Karel's ventures. Researchers were led through the often treacherous alpine reaches by local guides, an occupation that flourished in those times.

Going to the Source

From the time my 25-year-old daughter Julie and I first laid plans to visit Triglav National Park, we had heard about the origins of the beautiful emerald Soča River. Repeatedly we were told about how water seems to appear from nowhere before it turns into the rushing torrent that winds its way through Slovenia's green alpine valleys to the plains of Gorica, where it crosses what is now Italy and then pours into the Adriatic Sea. Like a sword in stone, the notion of water bursting from rock held an almost mystical allure, particularly since the little stream goes on to become a 100 mile-long river and then joins the sea.

We had started our Triglav adventure burrowing through the Alps behind a locomotive on the car train and reached the National Park's lodge at Trenta by evening. The next day as we drove up the road beyond Trenta, a sign to river Soča source trailhead jumped out at us. There was nothing to do but follow its direction. We soon found ourselves in a parking lot by the river near a trail leading upward. My knees wouldn't let me think of hiking the steep rock steps, but Julie didn't hesitate. She disappeared up the forest staircase as though reeled in by an invisible line.

It was already late in the day and the rain had gotten to be more than a mist.

No one was around. No sound penetrated the grey haze. The weak light began to give out completely.

Edelweiss (Leontopodium Alpinum)

The tourist road at Mangart, 2679 m, the Julian Alps

Mojstrovka mountain chain, Julian Alps

Julie didn't come back.

The rain grew more insistent. I waited. Then I waited some more.

Finally I girded up against the October mountain air, grabbed my walking sticks and launched myself into serious hiking mode.

The Truth about Triglav

The dragon was slain by Jason
In a fabled mighty conquest,
But to reach the Ljubljana Basin
The beast must have come from the west.
Now the Julian Alps,
With many distinctive a feature,
Attest to the storied encounter
Of Jason, the fleece and the creature.
A clearly discernable form,
Imprinted in alpine relief,
Depicts a monstrous mouth
That opens wide to the east.
Triglav's highest peak,
Fast on the upper snout,
Marks the great grey furnace
Where fiery flames blazed out.
Water that formed into clouds
As the vast head of steam blasted forth
Rained back on the reptile's head
And left seven lakes in the north.
You can still see the monster's eye socket
Where the Soča gives name to a town,
And Lake Bohinj now glistens
Where its bright blue tongue went down.

Finding SLOVENIA
A Heart and Four Corners

I had not quite crossed the river when down the trail, with a very determined gait, came the hiker. As soon as I saw her face I knew she had done it. She had, in fact, gone all the way to the source, dug her feet onto the slippery, tiny iron rungs protruding from the shear, massive rocks and pulled herself along by skinny steel cables.

Inching from rock to rock, feeling for the rungs with her feet just a hair's breadth above the water, she had seen the Soča spring from bare rock. Not only that, but she could peer through the cleft in the stone walls to where the mountain plunges down into the great green expanse of the valley miles below.

As I had been waiting for her in the parking lot, listening to the rain splash against the car windows, I had imagined her there. I considered who else might have made that same trek, maybe not on today's hiking trails, but on some pathway, barely visible, that somehow keeps leading you onward. Julius Caesar had probably walked that very passageway. The Alps are named after him, after all, and he is said to have cherished the area. I could picture him, like Julie, being led up the trail by some intangible force, breathing in deeply the crisp mountain air, listening to time and hearing the future.

A History of Guides and Authors

The end of the 1800s saw increasing alpine tourism and a growing need for guides that continued until the First World War in 1914. Locals from the towns of Trenta, Mojstrana and Kranjska gora, in and near the present Triglav National Park, supplied the greatest number of guides, and in 1906 the first Slovenian course for guides began in Ljubljana. Today's hikers have these early pioneers to thank for the extensive network of trails in the national park.

During this era Julius Kugy wrote several books that publicized the beauty and significance of the Alps. The legend of Zlatorog began from this period as well. The mountain club Dren added to the cultural interest of the time with photography, cave exploration and writing, including a mountain guide in 1913.

The National Park continues these traditions by publishing extensive informational materials and exhibiting photographs in its Bled headquarters. Rangers knowledgeable in natural sciences conduct tours and give presentations in the museums. Park policy encourages the employment of locals, so many of them possess a keen understanding of their region and will gladly share it with you.

Song of Julius

Soaring white mountain walls,
Steaming broth, frothy brews,
I drink it in.
Majestic cliffs send back a sound
and mingle it with calls of owls.
I will follow the stream on a
    path trodden through time;
its beauty and its past lead me
    to the source that,
like my heart,
springs from solid rock.

On a clear day in Ljubljana you can look down the main street and see the soaring Alps. The Kamnisko-Savinjske Alps to the north beckon the locals all year long. Although the services in these mountains are not as developed as they are in Triglav National Park, the rugged beauty and lack of crowds draws many natives. Krvavec remains a favorite for down-hill skiing and Velika Planina for cross-country. From Kamnik hikers fan out into the surrounding hills. Logarska Dolina's green meadows attract horses and its natural beauty lures artists.

Young ibexes

The Legend of Zlatorog

Once upon a time a poor hunter from Trenta fell in love with a rich girl. As a way to get money to woo her, he stole up the mountain to the home of a mythical Golden-Horned capricorn who tended a hidden garden of wondrous beauty. Knowing that the animal guarded hidden treasure, he stalked and shot Zlatorog. The animal fell from a cliff and died.

From the capricorn's blood that spilled onto the ground sprang the Triglav flower, restoring both life and magical powers to the animal. Furious, Zlatorog killed the hunter and destroyed the secret garden. The Alps sprang up from his wrath, and the treasure remains hidden in the mountains until this day.

First published in a Ljubljana newspaper in 1868 by Karel Dežman, the story of Zlatorog later inspired a poem by Rudolf Baumbach in 1877. The Slovenian translation a few years later, and a dramatization in the early 1900s furthered its popularity. The story became known throughout the Trenta-Triglav region.

Triglav valley lakes

Coming into Kamnik

The clock ticked quickly past midnight on the cold snowy March night that my husband Blair and I came into Brnik airport. We had picked up the rental car and made our way out to the Snovik thermal spa resort snuggled against the Kamnik mountains. Now, with not one soul stirring in any of the farmhouses we'd passed between Brnik and Snovik, we climbed around the brand new apartments on the hill wondering what to do. Obviously, I had neglected to request special arrangements for our off-season late arrival. No one broke the crisp stillness to hand us a key.

Exhausted from our boundless day of car and plane rides, from California to Frankfurt to Paris to Brnik and now Snovik, we preferred not to thread our way to Ljubljana only to return early the next morning. It made more sense to go back to the closest town of Kamnik and look for signs of life there.

As we approached, we began seeing ads for rooms and tried, in our somewhat confused state of minds, to follow their direction. Within a few minutes we found ourselves in front of a gostilna where a lamp burned cheerily at the front door. Near the light we eventually spied a button and debated whether at that time of night, by now close to 1.30 am, we would dare to disturb anyone.

With the thought of another hour's drive to Ljubljana as a strong incentive, we pressed the buzzer. Within about two minutes the second story shutters above us flung outward and a figure clad in a white nightshirt surveyed the scene. Apologizing for the intrusion,

The Kamnik-Savinjske Alps

I attempted to explain our plight. "Samo trenutek" – "Just a second," came the quick response.

The shutters closed. Within about 4 minutes the front door swung open with a completely dressed young man on the other side. "Kar naprej, prosim" – "Please come in." Just for one night, we answered, and, yes, we do have a car. In response to my apology for waking him up at that unearthly hour, the fellow looked at me and said a Slovenian equivalent of "that's why we're here." Within minutes Blair was driving through the high gate that our host had pushed open and then tightly secured behind us.

Putting the body to bed had rarely felt so fine. By first light we arose refreshed from a great sleep. While Blair dealt with business by phone, I wandered about and watched Kamnik wake up. Some residents were heading back home already with fresh bread, while others in long dark coats and hats fetched their cars from nearby garages.

That hour I fell in love with Kamnik. In the morning's gentle light, as I looked down from the little castle on the hill ringed by lacy snow peaks, I knew I was not the first. The mountains seem to wrap their great arms around the little place and history has crafted enchantment into its design.

As wonderful as Snovik's new hot springs resort turned out to be the next night, fate did us a favor by giving us Kamnik the first one.

Kamnik

The Southwest

The southwest's riches range from eye-dazzling sunny seashores to unseen marvels hidden deep beneath the landscape.

A Coast tied to antiquity. Piran, Koper and Portorož portray their Greek, Roman, and Venetian pasts. With a Mediterranean flare, they share sunny traits of pastel paint, fresh fish dishes, figs and olives. Their climates are tempered by warm waters, and their access enhanced by primeval waterways.

Hollow rock - the Kras phenomenon. A few miles from the ancient coastal towns you will find world-famous caves. Open as a tourist attraction since 1819 by Austrian Emperor Franz Ferdinand, Postojna Caves contain 12 miles of subterranean passageways. The discovery of "the human fish," Proteus Anguinus, prompted the study of cave-dwelling species as well as the science of speleobiology. The UNESCO World Heritage Site of Škocjan Caves is located in the regional park with trails and informational placards. In the town of Cerknica, a disappearing lake has fascinated scientists and emperors alike for centuries.

Old wines, white horses and quicksilver. Just beyond the Kras region, as the rocky grey terrain is known, the scene changes to vine covered hills. Goriška Brda near Nova Gorica and the Vipava region along the river valley both produce high-quality wines, and have done so for centuries. The Lippizaner horse country, with its white fences running through green trees and meadows, occupies a prime spot just in from the coast.. Further inland still the town of Idrija has placed an award-winning technical museum in its castle, has opened its former mercury mines for public tours and continues to produce hand-made lace.

Good connections. The road from the Austrian border in the north now quickly connects the mountains to the sea.

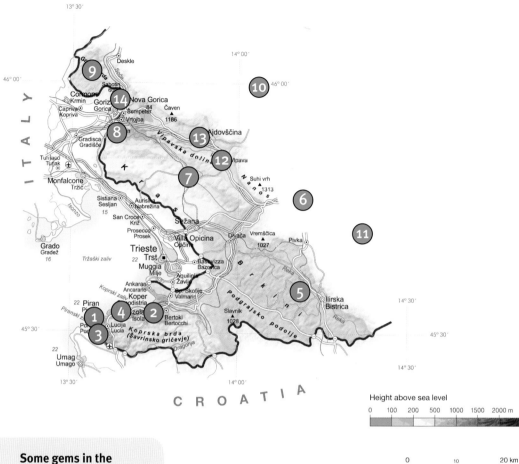

Height above sea level

0   100   200   500   1000   1500   2000 m

Scale   0   10   20 km

Some gems in the southwest

1. Piran
2. Koper
3. Portorož
4. Izola
5. Škocjan
6. Postojna
7. Štanjel
8. Lipica
9. Goriška Brda
10. Idrija
11. Cerknica
12. Ajdovščina
13. Vipava
14. Nova Gorica

Natives will tell you that they can ski in the Alps in the morning and swim in the Adriatic by afternoon. Indeed, a high percentage of the population does both with a fair amount of frequency, if not all in the same day.

Even though the coastline measures only 46.6 kilometers, or around 30 miles, the small towns hugging the shore have a big perspective on the world.

Slovenia's coast has received foreign ships into its harbors probably since boats have been afloat. Piran, for example, has been a port town under Greek, Roman, Venetian and Austria-Hungarian rule.

Strunjan

The coast reflects its long history with Italy. Stucco buildings with red-tile roofs and shuttered windows stand side-by-side along winding roads that lead inward into town. Fishing boats full of nets and floats line the edges of the harbors' turquoise waters.

Izola

Lake Cerknica

Locations along the coast still connect seafarers easily with other Adriatic ports, encouraging a constant stream of visitors. Architecturally, esthetically and culinarily, Piran and Koper in particular offer travelers a rich experience. Preservation of their unique heritage has kept both towns ideal for seaside dining and promenades, as well as fascinating walks through narrow old streets with little shops tucked here and there.

Historic home to Illyrians, Celts, Greeks, Romans, Celts, Slavs, Franks and Byzantincs, Piran found itself in the middle of a struggle in its Venetian era. Koper and Izola rose up repeatedly against Venetian rule, which began in the 13th century. Piran, however, sided with Venice in its struggles with Aquileia and Genoa for control of the coast. Venice was Piran's best customer for salt.

"Piran" may derive from the Celtic "bior-dun" meaning settlement on the hill, or from the Greek "pyr" for fire, stemming from the times when a lighthouse marked the way for Greek merchant ships. The town's layout dates back to the Middle Ages.

Koper in Antiquity

Conger up
Narrow paths
Winding between two-storey, terracotta-colored stucco walls.
Down at the very end
You catch a snippet of sea blue
That thousands for thousands of years have seen
And used, too, to sail to ancient Athens
Or to Troy or maybe Phoenicia
Or Alexandria.

Known to early Greeks as Aegida, Koper served as a city of refuge to Roman residents of neighboring Trieste's precursor city when they fled the invading Lombards. Renamed Justinople after the Byzantine emperor Justinian II, it later came under Lombard and then Frankish rule.

A trading partner with Venice since 932, Koper joined the republic of Venice in 1278. Along with Trieste, the city of Koper became an Austrian Littoral crown land in the days of the Austra-Hungarian Empire. Later it formed part of Yugoslavia.

Today the city is officially bi-lingual - Slovenian and Italian.

Aegida
Capris, Caprea, Capre,
Caprista
Justinople, Caput Histriae,
Capistrano.

Koper's past names

Koper

Koper

Portorož

The Port of Roses has long been a tourist destination for yacht owners. With a long promenade reminiscent of other European rivieras, Portorož hums with fresh fruit vendors, cafés, ice cream parlors, resort hotels and thermal baths. On the way out of town lies a regional park of ancient salt flats and marshes. At Sečovlje Soline Nature Park you can see a rich biodiversity of species and their habitats, especially birds, in a saltpan environment.

If you drive around the hills above Portorož, you'll come upon many small wineries, some with award-winning vintages, and an olive mill museum. Local gostilnas offer coastal and Kras specialties. You'll also find some great vistas looking down toward the sea.

The Lure and Lore of the Lippizaner

Lying just northeast of Trieste, Lipica has long been famous as the birthplace of the white Lippizaner horses that are featured in Vienna's Spanish Riding School. With its location just across the Italian border and near the Vipava wine district, it is also a short distance from the Slovenian coast and the UNESCO World Heritage Škocjan caves. Food, lodging

Lippizaner horses

and golf are available in Lipica along with horseback and horse-drawn carriage riding.

Škocjan Caves

Sink holes and caves riddle the Kras landscape in a region replete with mystery and surprise. Streams appear here and vanish there. The high limestone plateau reacts like compliant clay to the flow of water that wears, digs, and chisels the seemingly massive rocks.

Being both porous and soluble, the soft stone erodes into caverns, crevices, fissures, and intricate formations. In the 17th century, Baron Janez Vajkard Valvasor described it like this: "In some places one may see for miles, but everything is grey. Nothing is green, and everything is covered by rocks." The Baron went on to explain that the locals coped with the water shortage by producing good wines.

The highly unusual features of the area had been noted more than 2000 years before Baron Valvasor's observations. Fourth century Greeks told of underground tunnels and

Škocjan caves

UNESCO World Heritage Site

springs here, and Virgil wrote about the natural curiosities in his Aeneid. For ancient Greek seafarers the area was easy to reach, lying just inland from the ancient coastal cities.

Historians have long been puzzled by Kras, also known as Carso in Italian and Karst in German. In the 17th century A. Kirchner sketched an elaborate scheme of hydrophylacia, connecting karst springs to the sea by underground reservoirs. Court mathematician J. A. Nagel was sent by the emperor to solve the conundrum in 1748 to report on the "unusual and miraculous phenomena."

The universal geologic term "Karst" originates from this area, since this type of landscape was first studied and named here. "Doline," means depression in the topographical surface (swallowhole) and derives from this region too. In the Kras the dolines make homes for several species.

Apart from the wealth of scientific intrigue in the Kras, the region is rich in food and wine specialties. Delicacies born of adversity, the red wines here benefit from the dry summer heat and fierce 'burja' winds blow karst hams dry.

Since 1986 the Škocjan Caves have been under the protection of the United Nations as a site of world importance. With just over 3 miles of underground tunnels, some of them more than 600 feet deep and among the largest in the world, the caves serve as an international center of study for the karst phenomenon and the centerpiece of the Karst Regional Park.

By a system of cascades and falls the river Reka carves its way down to small underground lakes. Water that starts in the Kras drains through a system of underground passageways all the way to Timavo on the Adriatic coast, now in Italy.

Visitors to the caves can view stalactites, stalagmites, stone curtains, shafts, gorges, natural bridges, interconnected caves, canals and grottos as part of a conducted tour.

Postojna Caves

"Its enormous river galleries makes it one of the wonders of the world," according to A.C.Waltham in the book *The World of Caves.*

A number of archeological sites ring the caves. The area evidences continuous settlement from the Stone Age to the Iron Age, military fortifications by Romans and fortified villages in the Middle Ages. Archaeological finds here count among the most significant in Europe,

The Phenomenal Karst

Reservoir trees

With the way water escapes through the sieve-like kras rock, any vegetation here must hunt hard for moisture to survive. A tree stretches its roots as far down as possible, away from the bone-dry surfaces, and carries any residual water it finds back to nourish the trunk and branches above ground. The water that a tree loses through its outer membranes can prove vital to other growth, all of which clusters around the base of the tree, and even up into its branches.

Finding enough water to sustain human habitation has challenged Kras dwellers throughout time. Sisterns and catchments trap rainwater with elaborate schemes. All life revolves around the continuing quest for water.

Nova Gorica, a Highly Coveted Region.

At 18 years of age, the American author Ernest Hemingway (1899-1961) volunteered with the American Red Cross in Caparetto, now Slovenia's Kobarid. His experiences in the Soca River Valley, known as the Soca Front in World War I, heavily impacted his writings. The Soca River originates in the Julian Alps and runs through Kobarid on its way to the Adriatic, giving flat banks to an otherwise rugged topography. At Nova Gorica the river turns southwest and enters the plains.

Both sides of the war enlisted Slovenian soldiers in long, intense conflicts. The city of Gorizia is now divided between Italy and Slovenia, with Slovenia's side called "Nova Gorica." The Universities of Ljubljana and Trieste have jointly sponsored political geography studies in the area.

The picture on the preseding page was taken from the Kostanjevica monastery hill. Inside the monastery's crypts

Kostanjevica monastery above Nova Gorica

are buried the last of the Bourbon kings of France, Charles X (1757-1836), his family and his prime minister. Exiled and denied entry by Edinburg and Prague, the French royalty were taken in by a local aristocrat who housed them until their deaths.

The town of Nova Gorica was laid out according to the principles of French architect LeCorbusier.

Nova Gorica

Southeast

Slovenians will tell you that the southeast part of the country is the most genuine. Already in the thirteenth century its major settlement was being dubbed "New City," Novo Mesto. One of its other names was Rudolfswert, "worthy of Rudolf," after the founder of the Hapsburg Empire who gave the city its charter in 1365.

Romanesque. Lower Carniola

Stična. Lower Carniola, as the southeast was known, must have been a bustling place in the 1200s. Not only was the new city of Novo Mesto sufficiently important to warrant Emperor Rudolf's attention; the French Cistercians were undertaking the immense construction project of the monastery at Stična. Although more than seven centuries have passed since those vibrant years, the area as a whole has managed to maintain the tone of those times to a surprising extent.

Medieval estates. If you like the vaulted ceilings, outdoor passageways and rounded arches of the Romanesque period, a trip to the area will be worth your while. You will sense an ancient serenity at Sticna monastery. You can also see the secular side of those early medieval years in the myriad noble dwellings in the area, many of which are open to the public. Otočec Castle, holding its own in the middle of the Krka River, seems to have trapped and held part of the 13th century against the flow of time as well as water.

The business of fitness. Hot springs resorts with indoor-outdoor pools in park settings, herbal teas, and pharmaceutical medications interrelate under the sizable Krka Company.

Based in the southeast, Krka has become one of Slovenia's premier industries by incorporating several aspects of native lifestyle: outdoor exercise, nutrition and natural remedies. Krka is a name you will see often in the southeast: the river, the town and the business.

< Cross shaped hall in the monastery at Stična

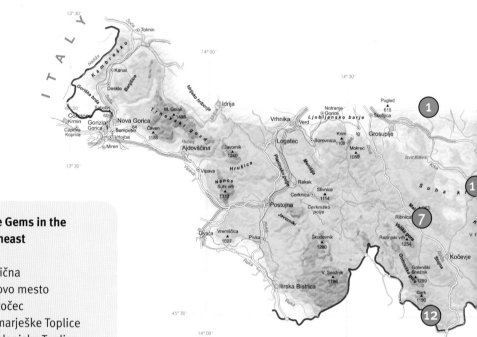

Some Gems in the Southeast

1. Stična
2. Novo mesto
3. Otočec
4. Šmarješke Toplice
5. Dolenjske Toplice
6. Bela Krajina (White Carniola)
7. Ribnica
8. Drašiči
9. Metlika
10. Brežice
11. River Krka
12. River Kolpa
13. Gorjanci

Country charm. Other genuine qualities of the area can be found deep in the countryside. Traditional songs and dances are still learned and performed by schoolchildren, especially in the White Marches, or Bela Krajina, known for its white birches and white regional costumes. The wines produced virtually in the entire southeast have also enjoyed a long, continuous history and carry with them the flavors from the past. Lahinja and Kolpa Landscape Parks lie near the Croatian border.

Stična Twelfth Century Romanesque

The French Cistercian monastery of Stična produced the 12th century illuminated manuscripts that were featured on Slovenia's stamps in 2004, and are now preserved in the National University Library in Ljubljana. Because of its distinguished Romanesque history, Slovenia counts among five European countries that belong to the Transromanican network of Romanesque Routes of Europe to promote a common cultural identity. Stična numbers among 25 Romanesque sites in Saxony-Anhalt and Thuringia in Germany, Carinthia in Austria, Province of Modena in Italy, and Slovenia.

Stična gained attention earlier in its history as well. Iron Age artifacts were retrieved from burial sites excavated in the late 1930s by the Duchess of Mecklenburg and are now part of the Peabody Museum.

Open to the public, the Stična Monastery contains extensive herb gardens and sells herbal teas and dried herbs.

Carniola, you may remember, was one of the several parts into which Ostmark was divided by the Holy Roman Emperor Otto the Great in 955, along with Carinthia, Styria, Gorizia, and the White March, or Bela Krajina. In the 800s the old kingdom of Carantania had become a Frankish border county, or "march," ruled by Bavarian counts. In the early 900s the Ostmark disintegrated after its occupation by the Magyars

The Charms of the Countryside

Folklore and custom

Like other regions of earlier realms, Bela Krajina (White Carniola) guards its local distinctions. One colorful custom involves "Zeleni Jurij" or green George, a young man who dons birch branches to symbolize the coming of spring. Evoking the spirit of the tree god in pagan ritual, he calls on officials to bid for prosperity for the people. Since Slovenia's independence in 1991, the Zeleni Jurij delegation makes the trek from Bela Krajina to Ljubljana to pay a visit to the President, marked by festivities in Ljubljana and the Bela Krajina.

Country custom also expresses itself in folk dance. Bela Krajina dances are the oldest in the country and reflect the Croatian influence, alternating fast and slow-paced segments. The Kolo from this region is the only round dance in Slovenia.

Ten regions of Slovenia each claim their own dance types and traditions. Themes often center on life's activities, sometimes reflecting the distant past. Wedding dance rituals, with couples kneeling on pillows, and shepherds' competitions on stilts come from different parts of the southwest. Mountain dancing of the northwest's Gorenjska is peppered with floor stomps, yodels, whistles and whoops. Lively paces and playful themes distinguish Štajerska dancing in the northeast. A Prekmurje dance in the northeast revolves around men leaving for the military, and reflects a Hungarian influence.

Trška mountain near Novo Mesto

Ribnica

Some 25 miles south of Ljubljana lies the little castle town of Ribnica, known throughout the entire country for its basketry products. Roving vendors from Ribnica take part in fairs and set up roadside stands with their baskets of all sizes and shapes hanging from the ceilings, stacked high on the sides. In September the natives return to Ribnica to sell at the fairs in their own town, along with local potters and woodworkers.

A "Riba" or fish is featured on the town's crest. Ribnica is the name of the nearby disappearing river that pops up

Museum of wooden crafts in Ribnica

southwest of the town, winds around a hill, flows east for a while and then disappears into the karst landscape. Before it vanishes the stream offers good fishing opportunities.

The town prides itself on some of its famous sons, including France Prešeren, (1800-1849), whose studies began here and the composer-musician Jakob Petelin Gallus (1550-1591), whose life began here. Another historic distinction of this early town lies with the peddler's patent, issued by Emperor Frederick III in 1492, that allowed untaxed trade throughout the Austrian Empire as it existed at the time. The special status was given to keep inhabitants from fleeing due to the persistent threat of raids from the east.

The castle, gardens and museum make an inviting stop. From there you can explore other karst phenomena at Cerknica, the disappearing lake, and continue to the caves at Škocjan. If you go east to Novo Mesto and the thermal baths at Šmarješke Toplice, you'll stay on small roads across some fairly high hills. Straight south you'll come to Kočevje, considered to be deepest Slovenia, where bears still roam and travelers have been barred until recently.

Brežice

At one of the furthest points southeast, Brežice is near a number of wine regions, thermal spas and the Croatian border, with Zagreb just beyond. The town's Renaissance castle guards a collection of armor, a festival hall richly adorned with murals of Greek and Roman themes, and archeological treasures. The castles at Sevnica and Mokrice lie a short distance down the road in either direction.

Finding SLOVENIA
A Heart and Four Corners

Staying in this area will allow you to explore it more fully. If you like to play golf, stay at Mokrice castle. For swimming, you might choose the restored Čatež Hotel and use their private indoor pools. Rogaška Slatina, a well-known mineral water bottler, therapeutic spa and producer of fine crystal, lies just about an hour's drive north.

Mokrice castle

The Northeast

Austro-Hungarian traces. Bordering Austria to the north and Hungary to the east, this quarter reflects influences of both parts of the old Austro-Hungarian dual monarchy. This is where sauerkraut meets goulash, literally and figuratively. Segedin guylas, a very tasty combination of Austrian and Hungarian national dishes, remains a favorite in this area.

Slovenia's oldest Roman settlement. From the oldest Roman settlement of Ptuj to modern thermal resorts, you have considerable choice of sights and activities within a small area. High mountain plateaux, rolling hills and Pannonian plains add geographical appeal.

Prekmurje, at the eastern edge. As elsewhere in Slovenia, you will find museums with local historical information. Consistent with their locations, the castle museum at Murska Sobota contains documents relating to the Hungarian influence; in Maribor the Austrian past predominates.

Ancient urban centers: Maribor and Celje. Maribor, Slovenia's second largest city offers many of the amenities of Ljubljana, but on a smaller scale. The third largest city of Celje, noted for the meteoric rise of the 15th century Counts of Celje, holds two of their castles.

Castles and parklands. Two castles due east from Ljubljana at the Croatian border have been renovated to different purposes. Mokrice serves as a hotel with a golf course and Brežice a museum. That area also contains the new regional park of Kozjansko. Several well-known wine-regions also fall into the northeast designation.

Cultural heritage. One of the most important archeological finds comes from this region. The situla, a metal bucket from the Iron Age, with detailed figurative relief depicting rituals and daily life, was discovered near the small

Some Gems in the Northeast

1. Maribor
2. Slovenske Gorice
3. Celje
4. Slovenske Konjice
5. Haloze
6. Ptuj
7. Ljutomer
8. Ormož
9. Mura River
10. Moravske Toplice
11. Murska Sobota

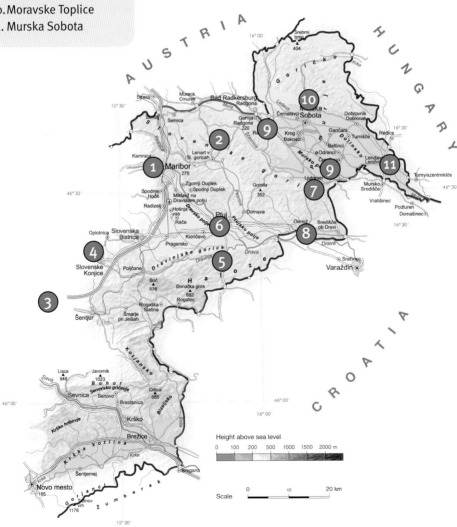

Fields around Ptuj

village of Vače. One of Slovenia's most distinguished authors hails from this region as well. Baron Janez Vajkard Valvasor lived in Bogenšperk castle about 40 miles east of Ljubljana. His book, a 17th century masterpiece entitled *The Glories of the Duchy of Carniola* continues to be the definitive work of the era.

Celje

Celje, the town on the way from Maribor to Ljubljana, had been only that in my mind until recently. Now river-walks follow the Sava, the market bustles with action. Within a short time Celje has become a town of sports events and festivals.

On the very first trip into what was Yugoslavia, Celje was our first stop. In the years since 1967 the town has undergone a vast transformation. Still a distinctive part of Celje's land-scape, the acres and acres of hop fields continue to be of major importance to the beer industry in Slovenia and beyond.

Two castles here have been renovated and are well worth the stop. The older one, with crenolations and walkways along the high walls, affords views down the Sava and across the waves of folded-rock hills. The one in town has a ceiling that is worth a visit in itself. The rest of the castle museum is very interesting as well, since nearby archeological sites have produced a wealth of artifacts from the Iron Age onward.

The river Drava
Beginning in the Carnic Alps shared by Italy and Austria, the Drava crosses southern Austria as the Drau and passes through the old capital of Carinthia, Celovec (now Klagenfurt) before it flows through the city of Maribor on its sweep through northeastern Slovenia.
After reaching Slovenia's oldest Roman city of Ptuj, the Drava defines the border with Croatia near the wine town of Ormož and then heads south to join the Danube.
It courses through some 90 miles in Slovenia alone.

Vače Situla

A fine example of situla art, the hand-shaped metal bucket found in the village of Vače is decorated with scenes from the Iron Age, or Hallstatt period, from about 90-350 B.C.E. The bucket, "seico" in the Istro-Venetian language, was used in rituals and was decorated by a method known as "toreutic," involving both engraving and hammering the interior.

A copy is displayed in Vače where it was found. The original is in the History Museum in Vienna.

From his meticulously recorded sketches, the countryside surrounding the castle where Baron Janez Vajkard Valvasor created his 15-tomed, 3,532-paged book with 528 illustrations and 24 appendices looks much the same as it did when he produced his masterpiece. His hunting lodge, a few folded hills away to the east, sits amid yellow and purple wildflowers against a backdrop of bright green trees on a deep blue-green sea of rolling hills.

In Ljubljana in 1641, Janez Vajkard was born to Jernej Valvasor and Ana Marija Ravbar. At the time Slovenian lands formed part of the Habsburg Empire. The "Carniola" that Baron Valvasor later extolled in his book "The Glories of the Duchy of Carniola" consisted of Upper, Lower, and Inner Carniola.

By age 17 the young Valvasor discontinued his studies to take a 14 year-long trip through Europe and Africa, during which time he joined the Austrian army. Shortly after his marriage in 1672 to Rosina Grafenweger, he acquired the Bogenšperk castle and there set up a workshop to write, print and publish his compositions. The expense of his endeavors ultimately cost him his castle, library and print collections, which he was forced to sell to pay off creditors. He is buried in Izlake, not far from his family's earlier castle in Medija, north of the river Sava near Trbovlje. The Glories of the Duchy of Carniola remains the major resource on the life and land there in the 17th century.

Marble monuments and painted glass reflect roots in Ptuj's hilltop museum, but the city's pagan past comes to the fore in an annual carnival to welcome the spring. It is then that masked figures surface from fields near the city to bring luck and fecundity to the locals. Wearing fearsome faces and clanging cowbells, the Kurenti, as they as known, chase winter from the land. You can see paintings of the fest by Maksim Gaspari and the one below by France Mihelič in the National Gallery in Ljubljana.

Vače Situla

Ptuj

From a castle-topped knoll, the ancient Roman settlement that is now Ptuj offers views across the river Drava Valley to the hills of Haloze. The flatlands surrounding the town of Ptuj remained rural after the railroad bypassed the town in the last century. Thermal baths and resort accommodations across the river are expanding. A pedestrian bridge links both sides.

Kozjansko

One of the newest regional parks, Kozjansko, offers a geological tour of 21 points. Plan about four to six hours to walk the path, about six miles in length. Publications on the park, produced in conjunction with the European Union, identify wild flowers and butterflies along the nature path in Vetrnik(about five miles northwest of Podsreda) as well as other cultural and natural attractions.

Nearby Podsreda castle dates from the 12th century and, despite Renaissance and Baroque changes, continues to be an important example of Romanesque architecture.

Prekmurje

"Beyond the Mura River" in Prekmurje, you will find the thermal baths of Moravske, architecture by Plečnik, and storks nesting above village houses. Great for biking, the terrain lies flat and paved paths usually keep their distance from the main roads.

Be sure to try the 'gibanica', a sweet specialty of the main town of Murska Sobota. Visit the castle museum for a history of Hungarian royal families and maps of Roman roads.

Gibanica - home-made dessert from Prekmurje

Sample Itineraries

5 days in Ljubljana, Center
1. Browse through the market, old town, and the castle.
2. Take an architectural tour. Visit the Stare Fužine Museum for Plečnik exhibits.
3. Visit museums and galleries.
4. Kod & Kam for maps and guides; attend musical or dance performances.
5. Walk in Tivoli Park; lunch at the garden restaurant in the park.

Stay at Mrak Pension or Union Hotel with a pool

3 days in Bled, Northwest
1. Walk or bike around the lake. Visit the castle museum.
2. Take a boat to the island and picnic there.
3. Visit Vintgar Gorge northeast of Bled.

Stay in the Grand Toplice hotel (high end) or one of many inviting pensions.

The Vintgar gorge, Bled

< Bridge over the river Soča

3 days in Bohinj, Northwest

1. Walk around the area at the north end of the lake and see the Ice Age boulders.
2. Bike and hike to the Sava Falls.
3. Take a gondola to Vogel Mountain and hike around Vogel.

Stay at Zlatorog Lodge or an alpine pension.

3 days at Trenta National Park, Northwest

1. Walk in the Juliana Botanical Gardens.
2. Visit the WWI Museum at Kobarid.
3. Hike in any direction and visit farm museums.

Stay in National Park lodgings near Trenta or in Bovec outside the Park

3 days in Kranjska Gora, Northwest

1. Hike, bike or ski the mountains around Kranjska Gora.
2. Visit the Zelenci Nature Reserve.
3. Follow the Vrata Valley from Mojstrana and hike up the back of Triglav.

Stay in Hotel Kotnik or pension.

3 days in Upper Carniola, Northwest

1. Visit the old town and museum.
2. Visit Škofja Loka and the castle museum.
3. Visit Radovljica old town and bee art museum.

Lippizaner horse

Stay at Hotel Bellevue on the Šmarjetna Gora hill; dress for dinner.

5 days in Piran, Southwest

1. Stop at the Škocjan Caves.
2. Walk up to the castle, to Strunjan along the bay. See the Lippizaner horses in Lipica.
3. Tour the other coastal towns of Koper and Portorož.
4. Visit the wineries in nearby hills, drink Teran in Teran.
5. See Sečovlje Soline Nature Park.

Stay at Hotel Piran (dress for dinner) or a pension.

Finding SLOVENIA
A Heart and Four Corners

3 days in Lower Carniola, Southeast
1. Tour Novo Mesto and the museum.
2. Visit Otočec Castle and the surrounding parklands along the river Krka.
3. Bike to Pleterje and the nearby villages.

Stay at Šmarjeske Toplice, or at a tourist farm.

3 days in Bela Krajina, Southeast
1. Tour the Metlika Museum.
2. Walk through the birch-fern forest to Drašiči wine village.
3. Visit Lahinja Landscape Park and Črnomelj for hilltop vistas.

Stay at Dolenjska Toplice with pools (dress for dinner).

3 days in the Pannonian Plains, Northeast
1. Visit the castle museum at Murska Sobota; eat gibanica in Murska Sobota.
2. Visit the Ljuotmer-Ormož Wine road.
3. Bike around villages and watch out for storks.

Stay in a bungalow at Moravske Toplice with pools.

3 days at Mokrice, Southeast
1. Visit the Brežice castle museum.
2. Visit the Kozjansko Regional Park.
3. Visit Čatež Toplice.

Stay at Mokrice Castle Hotel (dress for dinner).

3 days in Primorska, Southwest
1. Nova Gorica – Visit the crypts of the last French Bourbon kings.
2. Goriška Brda wine country or Vipava wine country.
3. Follow the river Soča up to Most na Soči and boat or windsurf on the lake.

Stay at a tourist farm.

The river Soča, the emerald river

3 days in Štajerska, Northeast
1. Maribor museums, Pohorja mountain and Lent river district.
2. Celje castle museums.
3. Slovenske Gorice wine district.

Stay at Dobrna Toplice with pools.

3 days in Logarska Dolina Landscape Park
Hike, bike and horseback ride all 3 days.

Stay at a tourist farm or pension.

3 days just North of Ljubljana
1. Visit Kamnik and the Arboretum.
2. Hike in the surrounding hills.
3. See Kamniška Bistrica or Velika Planina.

Stay in a thermal resort Snovik apartment or in huts on Velika Planina.

3 days in Dolenjska's Folded Hills, Northeast
1. Visit Janez Valvasor's Castle at Bogenšperk.
2. Hike up Mount Kum (gostilna at the top).
3. Visit Stična abbey, monastery founded in 1136 by French Cistercians.

Stay at a tourist farm or pension.

The Cistercian monastery at Stična

3 days in Ptuj, Northeast
1. Visit the castle museum.
2. Drive through the Haloze hills wine country.
3. Bike in the farm country around Ptuj.

Stay at a tourist farm, near Ptuj thermal baths, or pension.

3 days in Idrija, the Southwest
1. Visit the Castle Technical Museum.
2. Go into the old mercury shafts at the Anthony Mine.
3. See the disappearing lake at Cerknica.

Stay at Kendov Dvorec Manor House in Spodnja Idrija (up-scale).

3 days in Goričko, Northeast
1. Visit Goričko Landscape Park
2. Tour the two wine regions of the Goričko Hills and around Lendava.
3. Visit the historic thermal bath town of Radenci, of Radenska mineral waters

Stay at a tourist farm winery or pension.

3 weeks on Europath E6
Start from Radlje ob Dravi in the northeast and hike southwest on the European Footpath E6 to the Adriatic Sea.

Stay in huts and tourist farms.

3 weeks on Europath E7
Start from Kobarid in the northwest and hike south, then north on the European Footpath E7 to Hodos in the northeast.

Stay in huts and tourist farms.

"They are very friendly to their guests and they accompany them going from place to place and giving them all they want."

Anonymous 7th century author describing Slovenia's forbears

Customizing Your Travel

If you love to learn on the go,
stay physically active,
receive lots of intellectual stimulation, art and music,
enjoy a glass of good wine or beer here and there,
but also factor in time for quiet contemplation,
then I invite you, particularly, to read on.

With this guide and the internet, you have the tools to tailor your trips in your own style of travel. Start by defining your priorities. Set a general itinerary well in advance of your trip. Work with the web, maps and, I would recommend, Slovenia's official agencies.

Use the "Essence of Slovenia" section to obtain a sense of the country and see what aspects especially appeal to you.

Allot the total amount of time you want to spend and then break it down into parcels, based on your interests and needs. For example: "We have 2 weeks. We need 4 days without driving to get oriented, 3 days in the mountains, 3 days at a thermal bath where we can bike around, and 4 days on the coast."

Nail down your dates, preferably several months in the future for summer travel, and at least a couple months in advance for the off-season.

Make a list of your particular interests and needs. Include dietary constraints, special interests, percentage of leisure time you want, means of transportation, whether you prefer staying at a farm or in a luxury hotel - or what combination of the two - how often you'll need web access, how many opera and theater performances you want to attend, what proportion of time in the mountains to the seacoast or City, of hiking or taking the waters. As we did, you can arrange to have several different guides for various activities, and do the rest on your own.

Here are a few more contacts:

- Slovenian Tourist Board: *www.slovenia.info*
- National Park: *www.tnp.si, triglavski-narodni-park@tnp.gov.si*
- Ljubljana Tourist Board: *www.ljubljana-tourism.si*
- Bled Tourist Board: *www.bled.si*
- Kompas Tourist Agency: *www.kompas-online.net*
- Association of Historical Cities of Slovenia: *www.zdruzenje-zg-mest.si,*
  info@zdruzenje-zg-mest.si

Use the web for greater detail and to update information. Email the Slovenian tourist bureau to request brochures on subjects of specific interest to you.

Once you have a more specific plan, email appropriate agencies, hotels, etc. Most have websites, so you can communicate directly. For example, one scenario for the 2 weeks might be 4 days in Ljubljana, 3 days in Bled, 5 days in Bohinj, 3 days in Snovik. This itinerary keeps you within a small area of northern Slovenia. To be more expansive, consider something like 4 days in Ljubljana, 3 days in the Bled/Bohinj area, 4 days at the coast, and 3 days in Šmarjeske Toplice, or Dobrna, or Moravske Toplice.

Getting Around

Slovenia's airline Adria Airways flies to the capital city of Ljubljana from most major European cities. The airport lies just north of Ljubljana in Brnik, at the foothills of the Alps.

The train station is centrally located in Ljubljana, with good connections to the rest of Europe.

Buses run where trains do not.

Consider hiring local Specialists in Your Areas of Interest.

For the National Park, for example, you can arrange guides, itineraries and lodging directly with the Park. If rangers are unavailable, the Park can give you a list of other licensed guides. When my daughter and I took a 4-day tour in the fall, the Park helped us arrange for the car-train, ranger-led tours and a fully equipped new apartment at Trenta in the center of the Park. We enjoyed an invigorating time in magnificent surroundings that we could not have known on our own.

Slovenia's official website *www.slovenia-tourism.si* gives complete, current information on local attractions, dining and accommodations. Tourist bureaus can provide you with brochures and pamphlets covering particular topics, from horseback rides to historical landmarks. You will find the materials to be highly informative and well written, often by the University of Ljubljana faculty.

Here are a few key words, tips on pronunciation and techniques that can help you along.

Words You Need to Know.

Three essential expressions are "**Dober dan**," "**Hvala**," and "**Na svidenje**"

A Slovenian goes to get an eye exam for new glasses.
The doctor puts up the eye chart and asks "Can you read those letters?"
The Slovenian says, "Not only can I read it, but I know the guy."

"Good day," "Thank you," and "Good bye." You need these three because Slovenians greet each other constantly, and you risk being considered ill humored if you stay mute. For instance, when you step into an occupied elevator, say "Dober dan" and when you leave "Na svidenje." Even if you say it softly with no eye contact, it is important that you engage and disengage when you enter other people's space. When someone does something for you – from holding a door open, to giving you directions - you always thank them, "Hvala." Slovenians will usually embellish with a "sir" – "Hvala, gospod," - or "very much" – "Hvala lepa," but you can get away with a bare "thanks."

"Dober dan" is pronounced like "do" in dog with an emphasis on the "Do," "dan" is pronounced as it is spelled – "Dober dan."

"Hvala" is pronounced as it looks, with emphasis on the first syllable, and soft "a" sounds. But you do need to sound the "H" and "v" together, which is not easy at first.

"Na svidenje," the equivalent of "Auf Wiedersehen" or "Au revoir" can be divided into "Na" as in natural, "svi" as a svee sound, "den" as it is spelled, "j" as a "y" sound as in yellow and "e" as in egg, "Na svi den je." This will need a bit of practice.

Deciphering Slovenian

The language may seem daunting.

mrzlo – *cold*
zdravje – *health ("na zdravje" is the toast to health)*
vhod – *entrance*
slašiščarna – *confectioner's shop*
okrepčevalnica – *snack bar*

Here are three more.

"**Prosim**" – "please," pronounced "pro-seem." Say it if you want something, when you need to have something repeated, or in response to "hvala."

"**Da**" – "yes."
"**Ne**" – "no."

Don't ask for the bathroom. You may find yourself with a tub and towel. Instead, use "WC," (water closet) - "ve ce" in two syllables. Or say "toilette, "with a French accent. The Slovenian term for it, "stranišče."

Tips on Pronunciation.

Words are usually spoken as spelled. The pronunciation of foreign words tends to be as said in the original language, but

"železo" = iron
"postaja" = station
"železniška postaja" = railway station
"vlak" = train
"autobusna postaja" = bus station.

spelled out in Slovenian. "Eksotik," is "exotic;" "ambicija," "ambition." Mouth out the sounds and you may recognize something.

Three letters have the upside-down circumflex – č, š and ž. By itself "c" is pronounced "ts," as in "potica," like "pizza" with extra "o" and "t" sounds. It becomes "ch," as in "check" with the circumflex. "Črna Gora," Black Mountain, or Montenegro, sounds like "cherna gora."

The "s" sound changes to "sh" with the circumflex. "Še kaj?" literally "more of something?" asked often in sales transactions, sounds like "shay k-eye?"

"Z" as in "zebra" turns into the French "j" sound by adding the circumflex as in our "beige." These three are named after the whooshing sound the river makes.

Getting the Gist.

The grammatical structure is elaborate. Look for any piece of a word that you know, because it may have gained letters by conjugation or combination. "Dol" is down. "Gor" is up. "Dole pri Litija" means that the village sits low in the hills ("pri" means "near."). "Dolina" is valley. "Gora" is a mountain, "gorice" hills. "Kranjska Gora" is a town in the mountains near Kranj.

North is "sever, " south "jug" – hence "Yugoslavia, or South Slavia; east "vzhod," and west "zahod." Exit is "izhod" and entrance "vhod."

"Pot" is route or path. "Cesta" is road or "ulica" is street. "Auto cesta" or "autoroute" is a fast road, usually toll. If someone wishes you "Srečno pot" or "happy journey," you say "hvala, enako." - thanks, the same to you.

"Trst" is Trieste, so "Tržaška cesta" is the road to Trieste. "Postrv po tržaško" is trout Trieste style with garlic, oil and parsley.

"Dunaj" is Vienna, so "Dunajska cesta" is the road north to Vienna. "Dunajski zrezek" is Wienersnitzel. "Celovška cesta" is the road to Celovec, or Klagenfurt, Austria.

"Vino" means "wine, and "pivo" beer. "Sok" is juice, "sadnji sok" fruit juice. "Voda" is "water. "Pitna voda" means "drinking water. "Nepitna voda" is not for drinking.

"Kisla voda" is mineral water; "Navadna voda" translates to tap water. "Gaziran" is fizzy.

"Samopostrežba" (self-service) or "trgovina" means grocery store.

"Koliko stane? " means how much does this cost? It's pronounced as it looks.

Wish "lahka noč," a good night, as you retire.

The Gostilna

"Gost" means "guest" and "gostitelj" is "host." "Gostoljub-
nost" is "hospitality," with "ljubezen" meaning "love." You can
see that "gostilna" derives from the guest-host relationship,
and the love of entertaining.

A gostilna may have rooms for lodging, but not neces-
sarily. "Gostilna" usually is translated as "inn." Unless there
is a symbol for a bed, or some other clear indication, do not
count on being able to get a room there.

Serving food to wayfarers comes naturally - and historically - to Slovenians. Travelers have long depended on local
hospitality to sustain them along the rivers, across the plains,
over the hills and through the mountains as they crossed
lands that now are within Slovenia's bounds. Conversely,
the natives feel responsible for the wellbeing of their guests,
particularly when it comes to eating and drinking.

A Slovenian's signal of readiness to receive guests sometimes takes the form as subtle as the outline of a beer glass
on the window of what looks like someone's home, or even
a brightly colored roof. In other words, do not be afraid to
knock on someone's door if you think they may be serving
food. If they are not able to feed you, they can lead you to
someone else who can.

To someone unfamiliar with this understated style of
advertising, food can appear in short supply. Some friends
who were new to European travel had insisted that there was
nowhere to eat in the little towns around the airport. Once
we had passed sign after sign, I realized that they had been
looking for the exact words "Restaurant" and had dismissed
all other signage as commercial advertising.

Much of life revolves around food in Slovenia. The whole
village gathers in their inn, whether called a "gostilna" or
otherwise. In the countryside, a gathering at the gostilna
follows every seminal event, whether marriage, death, anniversary, or birthday.

Years ago I became aware of the importance of the gostilna when my cousin Pavla, who ran a gostilna with her
husband and sister, came with me on a trip to Serbia. In
a call to her husband about midway through the trip, she
found that a villager had died. From that moment on, we set
a course directly back home and she directed the preparations by phone along the way.

When we drove up to the gostilna, Pavla's sister handed
her an apron at the door and she stepped right into the operation as though she had never been away. Within seconds

she was seasoning pan after pan of meat slabs and push-
ing them into the wood-burning oven, as lettuce was being
cleaned, tomatoes cut, vegetables washed. Desserts had long
since been baked that morning.

We had first received the news down in Zvornik, Serbia,
some 60 miles southwest of Beograd. I had naively assumed
that Pavla would attend the funeral. It soon became clear
that preparing to receive the mourners far overshadowed
any thought of her appearance at the service. In less than an
hour after we came back from our trip, the deceased's family arrived and was seated first. Once the entire group had
gathered, all clad in long black clothing with the men wearing black hats and numbering probably 100 people, bowls of
soup began their procession from the kitchen.

Relatives from nearby villages had been summoned to
help in the preparations. The professionals could carry three
12-inch, nearly-flat bowls of steaming hot, parsleyed chicken
broth with fresh, thinly sliced egg noodles, all resting on one
arm. With the other arm they carried a fourth bowl, each
one resting on an underplate.

Once the soup bowls had been emptied and cleared
from the tables, out came the tender, juicy servings of veal

Tomato and vegetable soup

roast- "teletina" - crispy on top, with a perfectly rounded scoop of fluffy mashed potatoes on the side and a generous spoonful of meat juices over them. Next followed dishes full of "mešana solata," or mixed salad, portions of dressed escarole lettuce, quartered tomatoes and thin slices of red onions mixed with vinegar and oil, alongside marinated red beans. For dessert a slice of apple custard strudelj was brought to each diner. Finally guests received small cups of Turkish coffee.

Central to the success of the entire service is that the diner never feels rushed. Only the kitchen hustles.

Through the years that I have been privileged to witness the inner workings of the gostilna, the scene I have just described has been repeated many, many times. The kitchen pulses with preparations, but also with a steady stream of regulars who never come in the front door, but always through the kitchen. Each one receives a warm greeting and may even be enlisted into service if help is shorthanded.

Back in the early 70s before the village had a grocery store, I would see several huge metal jugs of milk arrive on the cart of a horse-drawn carriage by about 7 a.m. Anyone needing milk that day would cycle through the gostilna to fill their containers. Two little girls would ride along with their Daddy and be delivered to their school, the only one in a number of villages. In the early nineties after Slovenia became independent, everyone was anxious to tell me that a new school had been built in the village and it had a computer in every room.

With the early deliveries also came stacks of warm bread, all of which disappeared by mid-morning. Even today bread is carried into rural areas daily, now by "combi"- part van, part car – rather than horse and carriage. You can pretty well count on finding a fresh loaf in the morning, no matter where you are.

Spicy sausage used to be made by the "gospod" or master of the house, and sold along with other meats he had either butchered himself or bought from a local farm. He used to carry live chickens home in the back of his Mercedes and slaughter them behind the house. To carry the barrels of wine he would use his big flatbed truck and then store them in the cellar to dispense by the glass or bottle.

Fruits, vegetables and mushrooms would be brought in by the basketful from local gardens. In those days the gostilna served not only as the heart of the village but also as its distribution center for just about every kind of food and drink, including, surprisingly enough, bottled water. Two

Roast pork

types of mineral water have been around for as long as I can rememeber – Radenska, the green label with 3 red hearts, and Rogaška Slatina (both coming from famous thermal bath resort towns).

Even though you might not have a chance to see the gostilnas functioning now in quite the same way as you would have 30 years ago, they still play a key role in country life. In whatever part of Slovenia you happen to be, you may well find a slice of local life in a gostilna. If a band is playing, look for a bride or birthday cake.

Eating – the Perennial Passion

Having a meal in Slovenia means far more than a simple intake of food. To sit down to dinner equates to an act of friend- or kinship. You do it as often as you can, and always with good will.

The seasons drive Slovenia's gastronomy. You eat salad in summer, sauerkraut in winter. Inland in colder months you can find infinite inventive ways of using "kisle zelje," literally "sour cabbage." It is used with beans, potatoes, ham and sausages, as a soup or main dish. Closer to the Hungarian border, it combines with goulash for a reddish spicy dish called segedin golaž.

Winter's dark, cozy dining corners give way to summer's bright, open-air terraces.
You will be hard-pressed to see a 'gostilna' without outdoor tables anywhere from the Pannonian Plains to the Adriatic Shores.

Grilled sausage with cabbage

Restaurants will have menus, but in small villages the choice may be limited to what is on hand. If a roast is just coming out of the oven, that will be your best bet. Follow your nose.

Remember too, that lunch is the main meal of the day. Restaurants catering to tourists, of course, will offer a complete dinner selection. With gostilnas out in the country, though, expect to eat more midday and a lighter supper in the evening.

Apples, walnuts and cinnamon play starring roles in Slovenian cuisine because they are plentiful and keep through the winter in cold cellars. All year round you can find potica, the national favorite yeast bread filled in pinwheel fashion with cinnamon-spiced ground nuts. Apple strudelj is a sure sign of fall, although you can find it in other seasons too. In

Pickled cabbage with small pieces of fried pork

Finding SLOVENIA
A Heart and Four Corners

the east the apple štrudelj joins Hungarian poppyseed in a favorite dessert of "gibanica."

Skuta, a milk product that has no direct equivalent in the United States, finds its way into much of the cooking, baking, by itself, and even as a breakfast food. Probably the closest equivalent is tangy cottage cheese without the curd. It is used with fruit in strudelj, particularly cherry and apple, for a creamy effect.

Grains, plentiful year-round, play an especially important role in winter months. Cornmeal, buckwheat, even wheat flour can take center stage if properly prepared. One trick came back to me like Proust's madeleine when I saw our Slovenian relative do it recently. Without using oil, butter or even water, she poured flour directly into a pan and browned it.

If you are not familiar with this, you may be surprised at what a difference it makes to toast flour and then add your liquid – water, broth, wine, vinegar or a combination. The Slovenians use this method even in thickening soups and stews for a taste that is much more finished than plain flour. Hot, browned mush is broken down into bite-size bits by using two spoons to make little dumplings. Topped with cracklings, similar to crisply fried bacon, or dried fruits, or often with hot milk, it makes a meal in itself when the cold winds are blowing.

Other seasoning secrets come from the woods. Over 200 types of mushrooms are listed in handy reference guides, and must, under law, be collected in open-weave baskets so that the spores will redistribute underway. You are limited to no more than one kilogram, or 2.2 pounds at a time.

Grilled sardines

A fish has to swim three times
Once in the sea
Once in broth
Once in wine

Old Slovenian saying

Buckwheat (žganci) with small pieces of fried pork

Mushrooms, Herbs and Chestnuts

A Slovenian's feelings for mushrooms, herbs and even chestnuts, all seem to be portable obsessions, because my grandmother brought them across the ocean with her and my mother managed to transmit them to me. My mother used to lie awake on nights when the mushrooms grew. She knew the exact conditions that would cause them to shoot up within a couple hours' time. Even though I begged her to wake me up and take me with her on the hunt, inevitably she would be long gone by the time I even knew it. I could only hope that she'd find what she called a sheep's head and would have to come home to get help in lifting it. On one of her most successful excursions, when every surface of the house and outside tables and benches were completely covered with fungi, we had to call in someone to repair

Potatoes with mushrooms

something or other. The look on his face when he surveyed the scene I can only describe as awestruck.

Herbs and chestnuts also count big in cooking, although the hunt for them is not nearly as exciting as with the mushrooms. Parsley – the flat variety that Mother called "Slovenian parsley" and our Iraqi friend steadfastly maintained was "Arabic parsley," but usually goes by "Italian parsley," makes its way into soups, fish, stews and salads. Although preferred fresh, seasoning herbs are also hung to dry under porch roofs for wintertime use. Herbs for tea, like camomile and peppermint, are dried as a rule.

Dill, coriander, tarragon, bay leaves, basil, marjoram, oregano, rosemary, thyme, cumin, chives, garlic and paprika I know from my family, both here and there. On our first trip to Slovenia in 1967, my mother communicated in seeds, coming home with countless kinds of lettuce and flowers and sending back whatever she had not seen there. The Slovenians already seemed to have all the herbs we did.

In the fall on the streets of Ljubljana, warm smells of roasted chestnuts tame the crisp chills that announce winter. When the soft dark brown semi-spheres begin to drop to the ground, the woods teem with happy gatherers. Even on the road up to the castle, the trees yield their fruits to Sunday strollers and headstrong hikers alike.

Never in our experience in Slovenia, no matter how little people seemed to have, did we notice any shortage of meat, or any reluctance to serve it. Most prevalent probably is pork. Veal, chicken, beef, and wild game may appear about in that order, with the game being available in autumn. Fish is gaining in frequency inland. The coast generally, with its Mediterranean climate, operates somewhat differently, with fresh "ribe" – fish - and "sadje" –fruit - all year long. Increase in accessibility, though, is bringing more products to the Ljubljana market and inland in all seasons.

A Nation of Salad-Eaters

One reason Slovenia felt so oddly like home to me from the first moments must have to do with food. We couldn't speak, read or understand the language, but we certainly could eat. The way the food was prepared, I have later come to appreciate, bore a striking sameness to the way it was fixed at home.

With walnuts so plentiful in both places, so was potica, the ubiquitous favorite. This highly versatile nut-filled item lies somewhere between a bread and a cake that seems to go

Dandelion leaf salad with potatoes and eggs

with coffee better than anything else in the world – at least if you're a Slovenian. Every one of my aunts and grandmothers baked potica, not to mention my own mother, whose was hands-down the best in my mind. Mom packed hers so full of wonderful walnut-cinnamon filling that hardly any dough separated the nutty spiral from melding together when she rolled it up and baked it. Potica has been so important in our family that after my mother died, my father started making it.

When a big plate of potica was placed in front of us on the first time we came to the little village of Dole to meet our relatives, it was as though we were sitting at our own table, or my aunt's or grandmother's. The same held true for the taste of the salad, with its familiar proportions of vinegar to oil, and the way hot potatoes are combined with fresh lettuce to warm the flavors. Then there were the gardens.

People in Slovenia seemed to be as impassioned with gardening as my family in the States. Even in the middle of cities, you can see the patchwork of small gardens carefully tended by the residents of adjacent high-rise apartment buildings. Inside borders of bright yellow marigolds the beanpoles march in rows, and big round wire braces struggle to support sprawling plants heavy with ripe red tomatoes. Along the outskirts where they have plenty of room, cucumber and zucchini plants crawl, flower and bulge with long green produce. Fruit trees stand singly like sculptures and far enough apart so as not to shade the vegetable garden.

You can find dozens of varieties of salad greens at garden nurseries. A prime topic of conversation in the spring concerns first lettuce appearances and growth. Gostilnas pride themselves on their fresh salads, often combining salad greens with potatoes, beans and tomatoes for a composed "mešana solata." Dandelion greens are prized as a spring delicacy, and arugula (rocket) as a standard favorite. You will be hard-pressed to find a gostilna that doesn't offer fresh seasonal salad.

Potica

The way to tell a holiday was coming in our family was always by the rich, sweet, yeasty baking that heralded Thanksgiving, Christmas and Easter. By the time the kids rolled out in mid-morning on one of those school-free days, the poticas were already sliding out of the oven. By then the dough would have risen twice, been rolled thin, spread with a mixture that you hoped had not been completely cleaned away, twirled around, settled into loaf pans, and baked the better part of an hour.

As long as our grandmother was still alive, so was the discussion as to how soon we could cut into the bread. Gram

Easter goodies

Potica Making
Allot at least half a day for preparation and baking.

The Dough
Heat together until the butter melts
- 1 1/2 cups milk
- 1/2 cup white sugar
- 1/2 cup butter
- pinch of salt

Cool to lukewarm and pour into a food processor.
Then sprinkle on top
- 2 oz. dry yeast

Let stand for 10 minutes.
Mix in
- 2 eggs.

Then add and mix in
- Flour to make a soft dough, about 5 cups.

Place the dough in a warm, buttered bowl, cover with a cloth and raise it in a warm, protected area, preferably a pilot-lit oven, for about an hour. While the dough is rising, prepare the filling.

The Filling
Grind until fine
- 2 pounds walnuts
- 1 cup sugar
- 1 teaspoon cinnamon
- 1 teaspoon vanilla

Melt together
- 1+ cup milk
- 2 tablespoons butter

Mix milk mixture with nut mixture, and add
- 4 egg yolks

Beat to soft peak stage
- 4 egg whites

Fold beaten egg whites into nut mixture.

Punch down and roll out the dough on well floured cloth. Spread filling to cover dough. (Sprinkle with 1 cup of raisins heated in 1/4 cup rum, if desired).
By gently raising an edge of the cloth, roll the prepared dough into a pinwheel and cut to fit buttered loaf pans. To seal edges, cut with a plate rather than a knife.
Cover loaves with a cloth and place in a warm, protected area for about an hour. Bake at 350 degrees about 30 to 45 minutes. Let cool in pans for about 1 hour. Remove from pans and place on racks for an additional 1/2 hour.

Finding SLOVENIA
A Heart and Four Corners

steadfastly maintained that the yeast would keep rising in our stomachs if we failed to observe the requisite cooling-off period. Throwing caution to the wind, we children were never able to resist the lure of the steaming hot loaves. Once we cut into one, the rest of the family had no choice but to follow.

On the morning of the holiday itself, ham and hard-boiled eggs – colored ones at Easter - would accompany the potica. Our Mother would have had dinner preparations well under way as the family gathered at the table for the culinary entry into the main feast day. With the aroma of the turkey unmistakably in the air by the time everyone straggled together, the whole household paused to savor the simple, yet delectable, repast.

Slovenia Prizes its Fruit

Empress Maria Theresia (1717-1780), an "enlightened despot," instituted a program of planting fruit trees in her lands, including Slovenia. Fruit trees have remained deeply imbedded in Slovenian soils ever since.

"Sweet ice" can be found just about anywhere in Slovenia. From downtown Ljubljana to deep in the countryside, look for "sladoled."

Maria, the pear trees
  still bloom
Of seedlings from centu-
  ries ago
Three hundred years
  they've gone on
And still produce fruit
  comme nouveau.
An empress you were at
  the time,
Of the Hapsburg's sole
  woman to rule.
To augment the farms in
  your realm,
You used the trees well
  as your tool.
Pears and plums hang
  on the trees,
And apricots, apples
  and cherries.
Slovenia prizes its fruit,
And memories of you it
  still carries.

Cherries from Goriška Brda (South-west)
Fruit grows all over Slovenia. Toward the coast, cherries, figs, pomegranates and persimmons prevail. Inland you'll find apples, peaches, apricots and berries. Grapes grow everywhere.

Here are some favorite flavors

"jagoda," strawberry
"malina," raspberry
"višnja," sour cherry
"borovnica," blueberry
"breskev," peach
"zeleno jabolko," green apple
"oreh," walnut
" lešnik," hazelnul
"čokolada," chocolate
"Smetana" means whipped cream in the context of ice cream. It refers to other kinds of cream as well ("kisla smetana" is sour cream).

Slovenia's wine regions, concentrated in the east and west, are often referenced with two rivers and the sea:

Slovenia is famous for its high quality vines and wine.

Podravje by the Drava, Posavje by the Sava and Primorje by the sea. However, it seems that the only places you won't find grapes is where they can't grow - the Alps to the north, Kočevje's deep woods to the south, and the cities.

Each region has its favorites – Cviček in Novo mesto, Refošk in Koper, Teran in Teran near the Adriatic. Expect wines in the west to be influenced by Italian styles, and wines in the east to be more like Hungarian ones. The map below shows you the general wine-producing areas, but local agencies will give you a list of wine roads , maps and festivals. Check the web www.slovenia-tourism.si for official updated information.

"Wine is a food," my father staunchly maintained throughout his whole life. As I've looked around Slovenia, I see signs that everyone agrees with him. Wine must have been on my father's parents' minds as they came through Ellis Island, Pennsylvania and southern Illinois. I remember vines growing along the side of my grandparents' property not far north of St. Louis and a wine press commanding a prime spot in one of the many garden sheds. I think they carried the press with them all the way from the old country.

Smoked ham and home-made sausages

You reached the cellar under their old farmhouse by pulling up a heavy trap door. I still remember the damp, cool cloud that would rise from fermenting grapes from the depths when the hatch was raised. You could tell before you rounded the corner of the house whether it was open or closed.

My father continued the tradition. Part of the mystique involved growing the ingredients, like grapes or cherries. Otherwise you suited up in your rattlesnake boots, long shirt and pants in 100-degree weather and hunted the blackberries in your secret patch in the woods to produce a wilder, more exotic wine.

A visit to anyone's house always included a trip into the wine cellars, where you would taste and appraise the inventory. In today's Slovenia the custom still appears to be thriving. To escape a sizzling summer sun by descending into a cool cellar soothes the senses, even if you don't taste a drop.

Vines have been a part of Slovenia's landscape, surely for a good twenty-five hundred years. The sixth century B.C.E. metal pail discovered in Vače in the northeast prominently displays scenes of festivities involving wine. By the time the Romans controlled the lands, the vines could well have been established, leaving the Slavs to trim the vines when they left. Along with the Frankish King Samo's military assistance to the Slavic tribes in the 7th century there probably came the greatly welcomed Frankish viticulture as well. Undoubtedly in keeping with those long roots, today's wineries offer an extensive opportunity to savor the product.

Slovenia's burgeoning wine trade translates into a treasure hunt for tourists. This section deals with established wine regions. New intriguing ones await your discovery. Please forge ahead.

The country lies at an ideal 45°30'N and 47°N climatic zone, buffered by the Alps to the north and the sea to the west, with rolling hills full of microclimates, and wine traditions.

Slovenian wines are noted for being dry, fruity and well-balanced, but vary from Bordeaux-style reds to aromatic whites. Whites include the better known rizling, pinot, muskat, sauvignon, rebula, tokaj, traminec, silvanec, and the more unusual kerner, malvazija, pikolit, pineal, ranina, and rizvanec. Among the reds are barbera, merlot, cabernet, refošk, modra, šentlovrenka, žametna črnina, and teran, unique to the Teran area near the Adriatic.

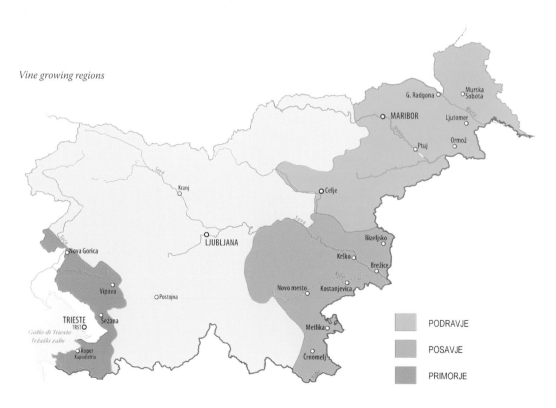

Vine growing regions

PODRAVJE

POSAVJE

PRIMORJE

Goriška Brda, perhaps the most widely known wine-producing area in Slovenia, comprises both cooperative producers of wines for an international market while small operations have artisanal style wines. The nearby Vipava area, to the south and east, and Kras just below it, produces an array of hearty reds.

Maribor in the north and neighboring Ptuj both are ringed with wine-growing regions of Slovenska Gorica, Ljutomer-Ormož and Haloze. To the southeast Novo Mesto sits in the middle of a large wine region, and the southeast-ernmost Bela Krajina area is known for its small wineries.

Out in the Parklands

Staying in small wineries can be arranged through tourist farms. Another option is to stay in town and make day trips.

Smoked ham factory at Lokev in the Karst region

Where to Lodge

Castles
Manor houses
Hotels
Apartments
Pensions
Tourist farms
Mountain huts
Hostels
Cabins
Camping
Sometimes room in inns

Your have a wide array of choices when it comes to sleeping arrangements. From castle to farm, you are likely to find clean comfort at the day's end. Staying in a variety of settings adds spice to your stay, although you will need to take along a wider range of clothes if you combine hotel and farm stays.

Top hotels can pamper you, although the small ones tend not to keep their restaurant open 24 hours. Room service can usually make up very nicely for lack of a full-time dining room, however. Pension normally means bed and breakfast, although there's often a bar associated with it where all day long you can get something light like a piece of štrudelj and coffee.

Gostilnas - inns - may have guest rooms, although not all of them do. Even if there is no sign for rooms or "sobe," the host might be able to accommodate you. If you ask, it is

Trenta Valley

likely something can be found for you, there or elsewhere. Remember that "gostišče" is another word for gostilna.

Even if you're camping in tents, cabins, or huts, you can usually find a nearby gostilna for your meals. Near Trenta in Triglav National Park I recently enjoyed fresh trout at a picnic table right near the stream where the fish had swum. Along with it there was local bread, a glass of wine, a freshly made dessert and coffee.

Thermal resorts typically offer hotel rooms, bungalows and apartments. If you're a day user, you can still eat at the facilities within the resort. Staying at the resort normally means that you have breakfast included and other meals too if you wish. If you choose full pension, often you will eat from the buffet in the larger dining room reserved for groups. This can be an interesting experience if they have theme meals, wines and entertainment from one of the areas in the country. Otherwise, you generally can order à la carte in a bar-café arrangement or in the formal dining room. Hotel staff can often steer you in the right direction in making the choice. Ask what they would do.

From Cabin to Castle

You can find hotels in the larger cities like Ljubljana and Novo Mesto and resort towns like Bled, Piran, Portorož, Koper and Lipica. Restored castles and manor houses can give you an equally elegant experience, with a country house atmosphere. Bled, Idrija, Otočec, and Mokrice are situated in wooded and gardened settings with many amenities.

Youth hostels dot the whole country. Ljubljana has a number of options for the younger crowd, including a well-located simple hotel. In towns with rail service, the train station tends to be within walking distance of some accommodations.

The following pages will allow you to see some of the choices.

Slovenia's Mountain Hut and Hiking Trail System

Alpinists, hiking enthusiasts, and casual walkers will all be delighted to find out that Slovenia has about 7,000 kilometers (4,200 miles) of well-marked and well-maintained hiking trails (poti, plural; pot, singular) that connect 162 mountain huts (koce or domi, plural; koca or dom, singular) providing drinks, food, lodging, and camaraderie. There are 53 mountain huts in the Julian Alps, 34 in the Kamnik and Savinjske Alps, and 13 in the Karavanke. The rest are scattered across various "hilltops" in the rest of the country.

In Slovenia it is possible to take both short day trips or longer multi-day trips totally on foot in complete comfort. Visiting or staying in mountain huts provides a means for meeting local hikers and sampling traditional Slovene-Alpine fare. For drink, try a warm, sweetened fruit tea (čaj), a cold Laško Beer (pivo), or a nice local wine (vino); for food, try ricet, a thick barley stew flavored with smoked meat, jota, sauerkraut soup, and štrudel, also called zavitek. It is relatively inexpensive to stay at a mountain hut in a dorm-style bunk using your own sleeping bag. Some also provide more private accommodation at a slightly higher price. As a visitor, your biggest challenges will be getting to and from the trails, either by private car, bus, train, cable car, and dealing with food and lodging negotiations in the Slovenian language at more remote huts. Plan your trip for unexpected weather conditions, particularly if you plan to hike at a high elevation.

Several resources are essential for your hikes. For both planning and hiking, you will need good maps that show the topography, trails, and mountain hut locations. These are available at a variety of scales. The mountaineering maps (planinske karte) at a 1:25,000 scale are the most detailed (e.g., Storžič and Košuta, and Grintovci). The 1:50,000 scale leisure series maps (e.g., Triglavski Narodni Park, Zgornja Savinjska dolina) also work well for hiking and give a nice broad view for planning. All of these maps are produced

Hiking path markings

Aljaž tower on the summit of Mount Triglav, the highest mountain in Slovenia

by the national mapping agencies (Institut za geodezijo in fotogrametrijo; Geodetski Zavod Slovenije) and are widely available, e.g., at the Kot and Kam shop in Ljubljana, as well as other scattered specialty shops around the country.

Lodging - Manor House and Villa

Kendov Dvorec and Vila Bled

Both the former manor house of the Kenda family near Idrija and former head of Yugoslavia Marshal Josip Broz Tito's estate at lake Bled have been accepted into the prestigious international Association of Relais & Chateaux. Judged on courtesy, charm, character, calm, and cuisine, both also qualify because they have at least a 4-star rating, a capacity of less than 100 guest rooms, and a quality gourmet restaurant.

Kendov Dvorec, a 14th century cultural monument in the 800-year-old village of Spodnja Idrija, commands a hilltop location just north of Idrija. Restored and furnished with antique, carved wood furniture, the hotel is decorated with local lace and imported fabrics.

Newly renovated, Vila Bled offers apartment-like accommodation, ideal for families and groups. With its twelve acre setting just across from lake Bled, the hotel offers privacy within close proximity to a variety of activities.

Relatively Speaking...

With Americans being as mobile as they are, our lives have been spent in many places. In our own family, my grandparents moved across seas and continents, and were further separated from their Slovenian relatives by two World Wars. My parents lived in several different states before settling in Indiana for 40 years.

For the most part, our relatives in Slovenia stayed close to home. When we came to Slovenia for the first time in 1967, my parents and I wondered how our relatives there would feel about us. My grandfather and grandmother had left their relatives at the turn of the 20th century, never to see them again.

It took hours on small roads with many stops for guidance before we pulled up in a tiny village tucked far into the hills east of Ljubljana. Once inside the gostilna, the proprietor strode up to Dad, who had marched confidently ahead of Mother and me. Searching for some way to present himself, Dad reached far back into his memory and, complete with explanatory hand gestures, pronounced, "Ti si Povše. Jaz sem Widmar," something in the order of "You Tarzan. Me Jane."

The air cleared completely. My father's cousin Tone greeted us warmly and led us back into the kitchen to present his wife Pavla, son Tone and sister-in-law Slavka

Years later we heard what our relatives thought about our entry into their little village of Dole. Dad's cousin Tone had taken one look at Dad coming in the front door of the gostilna and thought "Chicago gangster" because of Dad's hat. In our turn, we were paranoid about going into Yugoslavia and ready to see danger lurking on all sides. At first we even thought Tone was leading us away from the main part of the gostilna so that no one would see us or know we were there - as though driving around and around with German customs plates hadn't alerted everyone in the Sava hills that a visitor was roaming around.

We soon found ourselves being treated as greatly honored guests. As we sat at the kitchen table, Tone, Pavla and Slavka started bringing endless pitchers of wine and platters of food. Within a surprisingly short time a procession of relatives and friends made their way there to greet us. One told of bidding farewell to my father's father and his brother as they left for their long voyage to America. Another talked about what had happened to my father's mother's home during the war and how they rebuilt it. That day – and far into the night with music and dancing – we began to understand how the prodigal son must have felt upon returning home.

The following day we were taken on a tour of our relatives' homes. At each stop, we scooted onto benches around the table. Out came the finest wines, spirits, homemade breads, hams and sweets. The rules appeared to be that the more you ate and imbibed, the greater appreciation you showed. So as not to insult anyone, we ended up barely able to move away from the last table, just in time to be taken back to the gostilna for dinner. How exciting it was to see that relatives who had stayed in their little villages had thrived on their own terms. Conditions had improved somewhat in the 60 years since my grandparents left, but cars, for example, were few, small and far between in the 60's. Regardless of circumstances, people made the best of what they had. Any shortage of material possessions appeared to be offset by a gusto for life, land and family.

Leaving Dole that first time was a wrenching ordeal. We were given salamis, breads, wines, brandy, juices, wooden souvenirs and hand-crocheted doilies. In an attempt in some small way to thank our relatives for all they had given us, we attempted to slip some dollars into 9-year old Tone's hands. Big Tone, Pavla and Slavka were horrified. The constant quandary remains how to repay the extraordinary generosity we find in Slovenia.

On every visit since that time I have witnessed Slovenia's resilient good-humor. None of the distance, time and lack of communication that kept our families apart for so many decades seems to matter to anyone.